NEW YORK

SPANISH/ENGLISH TERMS FOR NURSES

D1611680

ED

Library of Congress Cataloging-in-Publication Data

Spanish/English terms for nurses. -- 1st ed.
    p. ; cm.
  ISBN 978-1-57685-696-3
  1. Spanish language--Conversation and phrase books (for medical personnel) 2. Nurses. I. LearningExpress
(Organization)
  [DNLM: 1. Medicine--Nurses' Instruction. 2. Medicine--Phrases--English. 3. Medicine--Phrases--Spanish. W
15 S735 2009]
  PC4120.M3S63 2009
  468.3'42102461--dc22
            2009016495

Printed in the United States of America
9 8 7 6 5 4 3 2 1
First Edition
ISBN 978-1-57685-696-3

For more information or to place an order, contact LearningExpress at:
2 Rector Street
26th Floor
New York, NY 10006

Or visit us at:
www.learnatest.com

Contents

The goal of this book is to help you communicate more effectively with Spanish-speaking patients in order to improve the quality of the medical care they receive. This is a much easier task than trying to teach you the entirety of the Spanish language. You will learn Spanish, of course, but it will be a practical form that doesn't delve into unnecessarily involved language rules. In other words, when it comes to Spanish grammar, if we didn't have to include it, it isn't included.

To help improve your bilingual communication skills, *Spanish/English Terms for Nurses* is divided into three main sections:

1. **Overview**—We'll provide tips to help you remember Spanish phrases, discuss various cultural beliefs you might encounter when dealing with Latino patients, and offer suggestions to help you understand your patients better and empathize with them.

2. **Spanish-Language Basics**—Here we'll cover pronunciation of Spanish words (which are actually much simpler than English) and other fundamental facts about Spanish grammar that will help familiarize you with the language. Whenever possible, we will step lightly over the rules of Spanish grammar. (Spanish does not have as many tortuous

rules as English, but it's got some tricky points.) Instead, we will concentrate on teaching you only the essentials of Spanish.

3. **Medical Phrase Lists**—The main portion of the book will provide Spanish translations for relevant phrases that you might need when working with patients who are predominantly Spanish speakers. Whenever possible, the phrases have been grouped together into categories, so that someone working in a pediatrics ward can find relevant phrases in the same place in the book. Throughout these sections, you will encounter an icon like this: 🎧 . When you encounter the 🎧 icon, the words and/or phrases that follow will be available for listening at:

http://www.learnatest.com/SpeakingGuides/

A GOOD APPROACH

The first two sections provide a framework for the third. If you already understand the basics of the Spanish language, and have an idea of how you would like to learn and employ the various phrase lists, then you can certainly skip those pages and jump straight to the lists. However, we recommend starting at the beginning as this is the best way to ensure that you get the most from this book. It's like putting together a complicated toy: You can just look at the finished product on the box and try to figure it out, or you can go step by step and give yourself the best chance of succeeding the first time.

After you get comfortable with the phrases in this book, you may want to continue learning Spanish; if so, great! If not, simply being able to help Spanish-speaking patients receive better medical care is a worthy achievement in itself. Latino people (also referred to as Hispanics) are the largest minority population in the United States, and more immigrants arrive each year from Spanish-speaking countries than anywhere else. Some already speak English, but many Hispanic immigrants arrive in America for the same reason people from all over the world have since the country was created: to make a better life for themselves and their families. By communicating with a patient in their native language, you can help them receive quality medical attention and respect their cultural origins at the same time.

THE GOAL OF THIS SECTION is to review some of the basic problems faced by Latino(a) patients seeking health care in the United States. We'll discuss how you can be an advocate for your Spanish-speaking patients, and we'll briefly explain how understanding and recognizing certain cultural differences can help you make your Spanish-speaking patients more comfortable and cooperative in a medical setting. To begin, let's talk about learning a new language.

RELAX: YOU CAN COMMUNICATE WITH YOUR HISPANIC PATIENTS

In 2006, the Latino Healthcare Task Force identified several areas of negative impact on the care received by Hispanics in the United States. Topping the list was the lack of health insurance, a problem faced increasingly by many low-income Americans of all races. Yet while a lack of sufficient funds to pay for medical expenses is a serious problem, it is not the sole one. Many well-educated, financially successful Latinos and Latinas (Spanish-speaking men and women) face the same ethnic barriers as those less affluent than them, due to cultural bias and the ignorance of both patients and the medical community that serves them.

To some extent, the inability to access quality care is due to a lack of understanding regarding navigation of a complex system. The language barrier limits the ability to ask questions, as well as knowledge of what questions to ask. In addition, a 2008 study revealed Latinos are less likely to undergo surgical procedures than any other ethnic group. Whether this lack of treatment is secondary to cultural mores or simply a misunderstanding of the necessity, the patient is placed in jeopardy because there has been inadequate education by the medical community.

The task force determined that one of the ways to assure adequate quality healthcare is to empower the Latino community to be better healthcare consumers and to partner with the medical establishment to reduce cultural and linguistic barriers. It is widely recognized that communication is essential for any progress in this arena. The fact that you, a healthcare professional, have this book in your hand shows that the right people are taking the necessary steps to increase the quality of healthcare in this country.

LEARNING ANOTHER LANGUAGE

You can learn to read and speak Spanish, even if you have tried before with little success.

While our intent is to help you care for Spanish-speaking patients and their families as soon as possible, we are confident that once the basics are absorbed, communication will be possible at higher levels. If you have tried before and did not learn Spanish, know that it was the method that failed, not you!

Before we get into any detail, let's eliminate a few misconceptions about learning a new language, be it Spanish or any other. There are an ever-increasing number of schools and advertisements touting immersion as the best way to learn. These groups say that you must "learn as the natives do" or "learn as children learn" in order to grasp Spanish, or that to understand Spanish you must train your mind to "think in Spanish." While immersion is an effective method of learning a new language, it is not necessarily the path you need to take to better communicate with your patients. You can learn to speak Spanish in your professional capacity without having to go to the extreme lengths required by most immersion methods. With this in mind, let's discuss the basic ideas that will help you better communicate with Spanish-speaking patients. Here is how this section is organized:

1. Preparing to learn
2. Understanding the basic nuances of the culture
3. Advocating for your patients
4. Working with parents and families of sick children
5. Making your Spanish-speaking patients comfortable

We'll cover each of these sections in the upcoming pages, starting with ways to learn a new language.

PREPARING TO LEARN

This section will help you formulate a plan to make the most efficient use of this learning guide. At its most basic, our program involves learning phrases—multiple words you can use right away.

Believe it or not, relaxation can greatly help you learn Spanish. Having a calm state of mind helps you absorb the language much better than when your brain is nervously flitting from one thought to the next. Here are a few ways to get in a relaxed mood:

› Trust that you can do it. You've already learned at least one language: You can learn another.

› Try deep breathing exercises: Close your eyes, breathe through your nose into your abdomen, hold it for a few seconds, and slowly exhale through your mouth.

› Give yourself time to learn! Don't rush it or try to cram, as these will make you tense and impede the learning process.

› Have fun. Don't become discouraged if you have trouble with pronunciation or use the wrong word; laugh about it instead of being embarrassed, angry, or depressed.

Most people stumble and panic when they think language is all about dissecting sentences and learning tenses and participles. Fear not! Learn in patterns and everything will fall into place.

Through this book you will become familiar enough with Spanish to become a competent communicator with your Hispanic patients. There are a few thoughts you will need to keep in mind.

> Learning a new language is a process, not an event. You're not going to speak the language from day one, but there are ways to make the transition and be effective while learning.

> Not everyone who speaks Spanish has the same cultural background or accent.

We'll try to cover some basic differences in this book, but it will take some time to comprehend all the differences between a speaker from Spain and one from Argentina.

> When trying to communicate with a non-English speaker, try to speak clearly and slowly. Never yell, as it doesn't make your words any easier to understand.

THE LEARNING PROCESS

It's said that a person needs around 150 words to make basic communication work. Add a few more words for a specialty field (like health care), and you can start interacting successfully with your patients by knowing about 250–500 words. Chances are good you're already familiar with some Spanish words, as you have undoubtedly heard some of the most frequently used terms spoken on television, in a film, or by people in your community. This means you already have the beginnings of a Spanish vocabulary without realizing it. For instance, medical professionals frequently ask questions involving basic words like:

> **What:** *Qué* (What is your name? What day is today? etc.)
>
> **Where:** *Dónde* (Where does it hurt? Where did you get hurt? etc.)
>
> **Who:** *Quién* (Who do you live with? Who is your doctor? etc.)

> **Why:** *Por qué* (Why are you here? Why don't you eat? etc.)
>
> **How:** *Cómo* (How many children do you have? How did this injury occur? etc.)
>
> **When:** *Cuándo* (When did the pain start? When did you take the medicine? etc.)

In normal conversation these words are prevalent. Putting them together just takes time and practice. Unless you have a photographic memory, it's going to take a few weeks or months to master vocabulary and phrases. A great way to get started is to go through the phrase section and check out which ones have the most application for your field. In other words, if you are working on a neurology floor, it is unlikely you'll be instructing patients to keep weight off of an ankle cast, or explaining to a new mother how to burp a baby.

Getting the vocabulary down should be viewed as a bump in the road, not an insurmountable hurdle. We've found a few easy methods that have worked not only for language development, but also for retaining important facts and figures such as measurements, formulas, and drug actions/reactions. Be warned: The first method might bring back memories of junior high.

IT'S IN THE CARDS

First, get some plain, old-fashioned 3 □ 5 index cards (even in the twenty-first century, stores still carry them). Then select ten statements or more from the phrase lists; put the Spanish on one side and the English on the other side. You can use these cards to practice with. If you are with a patient, you can ask the question and if the patient does not understand, the Spanish side of the card can be shown to them.

Read and use the cards frequently at work, even if the patient can speak English. When at home, place some cards in strategic locations: on mirrors, kitchen cabinet doors, or anywhere they are in direct view. If you're feeling especially arts-and-craftsy, make a poster-sized list of Spanish-to-English phrases. (If you have young kids, they would probably enjoy decorating the poster for you.) This poster, printed and mounted somewhere in your bedroom or bathroom, can be more beneficial than you may imagine.

Just seeing the content all the time, especially when you are relaxed, will be surprisingly effective, even if you don't make a specific point of committing the phrases to memory.

If you think this idea is not worth the effort, consider the billboards and other advertisements you see daily. Few people spend time memorizing the ads they see on their way from one place to another; after a while, however, the words sink in. With ads, it often takes only a few days before you know what they are selling and can repeat the text. The concept is the basis of Madison Avenue advertising.

In the beginning, use the phrase cards when appropriate with your patients. Read the question or statement to them. If they don't understand, don't get frustrated. Ask them to read the question and say it out loud.

You could say:

> ¿Favor leer esta pregunta en voz alta, lentamente, así puedo aprender la manera correcta de pronunciar las palabras?

...which means:

> Would you please read this question out loud, slowly, so I can learn the correct way to pronounce the words?

Most patients will gladly assist and also appreciate you are making an effort to comfort them.

In addition to placing questions on index cards, you can also place common responses on cards in both Spanish and English. Creating cards that have common responses to some questions can also be very helpful, both for you and the patient. Having the patient say the phrases in Spanish will help train your ear to that language. You could ask the question and then say:

> Por favor elige una de estas respuestas
> y dígamela lentamente.

Please pick one of these answers and say it to me slowly.

Listen carefully to how they pronounce the words. Each patient will probably sound a bit different.

When you write your cards, come up with as many possible answers as you can think of, since you never know what the response will be.

Study the questions and answers on a set of index cards until you recognize all of them. Then create a new set of cards, incorporating them with the first if you like.

SPANISH DIALECTS

There are cultural and regional differences among the various Hispanic groups that may affect their accent and phraseology (how they construct sentences). It's not very different than someone in Vancouver trying to understand a native of Tennessee. You will quickly understand there are multiple dialects, but they are not too hard to grasp. For example, consider something simple, like how to say "thank you." The Spanish word is gracias: some pronounce the c like an s, but others pronounce it as th. That's one clear difference, but it's not too hard to overcome with a little practice.

MORE WAYS TO INCREASE YOUR KNOWLEDGE OF SPANISH

Index cards are a very effective way to learn

Spanish while on the job, but they are not the sole means you should employ. If possible, try at least one of the following methods to increase your familiarity and comfort with the Spanish language.

Watch Spanish Television

New Spanish speakers sometimes have their confidence shaken when they can't understand responses, mostly because native Spanish speakers talk at a rapid pace, far faster than new learners can comprehend. This is where your local satellite or cable company can help. There are many Spanish-speaking channels available in the digital TV universe. People with access to international programming can get broadcasts from Mexico, Dominica, Cuba, and Puerto Rico. There are also a number of Spanish channels right here in the United States. Find a show you like and watch it!

SPANISH ON THE RADIO

Listening to Spanish songs and Spanish radio programming can also be beneficial, but in the early stages of learning the language it might not be as helpful as watching a TV show. This is because with a show, you have visual signs and other contextual clues to help you understand what is going on and what is being said.

For someone just starting out, listening to the radio will help you understand the rhythm and pronunciation of some words, but it might not be very easy to figure out what is being said. Once you get better at Spanish, however, the radio provides a nice challenge, especially for someone who can watch a television show and pick up most of what is going on.

You will find a slower pace with children's learning programs, as opposed to cartoons, but take your choice. Soap operas may be particularly beneficial, especially if they have a medical theme. When listening, don't rely on your dictionary or phrase book: Try to figure out the meaning from the context of the conversation. Advertisements are also helpful since you will probably recognize many of the products and slogans, making it easier for you to translate.

Your skills will also be enhanced by watching the programming from more than one country if possible. The country that offers the best shows for you depends on where the bulk of your patients come from. In a place like New York City, there is a rich blend of nationalities, while a city like Albuquerque has a Hispanic population that is predominantly Mexican. You can learn the language from any of them; just be mindful different characteristics exist.

Spend some time identifying common words. You will find yourself picking up the grammatical context as your skills grow.

Eat at Hispanic Restaurants

Look at a Spanish menu and get comfortable ordering in the language. It's best done in a Hispanic neighborhood where the clientele principally speak Spanish. You'll soon learn to recognize common idioms.

Attend Spanish Worship Services

If you live in a big enough city, chances are

good you can find a Spanish language church service in your denomination. Since you're probably already familiar with the content, the transition should not be difficult and will improve your ability to recognize vocabulary and sentence structure.

Get Help from Your Friends and Coworkers

People who already speak Spanish are usually happy to oblige neophytes. Your friends will also want to help you accomplish your goal. Sometimes we learn the most when we attempt to teach; here is an opportunity to improve your breadth of knowledge by teaching one or two friends and speaking to one in the language.

Ask Your Hispanic Patients

Patients who are not too ill to communicate often welcome the opportunity to help language students (it also provides an occasion to laugh most of the time!). People frequently feel guilty asking others for assistance, especially when they are ill. Asking a patient's help may be doing them a favor.

Find a Spanish Crossword Puzzle Book or Other Publication

Granted, this may be a more advanced step, but it is something to keep in mind as you progress. If you have access to a *bodega* (a Latino food market), you may find a few children's books or word games. You're also sure to find magazines. Some of the larger chain store bookstores also carry publications of all kinds in major languages.

And no, Spanish sudoku does not count.

Listen to Yourself

If you own a computer, it likely has the ability to record and play back speech. You can also use a digital or other recording device to listen to your own pronunciation. Do you understand what you said?

Label a Picture of the Body

Using a preprinted or hand-drawn picture of the human body, label in Spanish the major organs your particular specialty focuses on. If you are a generalist, then label major areas such as the head, neck, heart, stomach, and so forth. Study the picture, just as you do your index cards.

> One word of advice here: Be sure to differentiate between stomach and abdomen. Many patients of all ethnic backgrounds will say "stomach" when it is the abdomen that is the problem.

Of course, you don't have to do every one of the ideas listed here, and you may find a method not mentioned here that you enjoy. So long as you devise a course of action that works well for you, the particulars do not necessarily matter.

UNDERSTANDING THE BASIC NUANCES OF THE CULTURE

Knowing about your patient's culture can go far in understanding their reactions as well as their perceptions. Spanish-speaking patients in North America are most often from one of the following places: the Canary Islands, Costa Rica, Cuba, the Dominican Republic, Ecuador, Mexico, Puerto Rico.

In general, it is best to ask the patient where they were born rather than saying something like, "You were born in Puerto Rico, right?" To do so may very well insult the individual if they hail from somewhere else. Most people—not just Hispanics—are proud of where they were born and find being labeled as from another area an insult. Ethnic rivalry can be quite im-

portant in the Hispanic community. (Note that the word is rivalry, not prejudice.)

Many Hispanics have tight-knit, extended families, and they can be quite helpful in learning about the patient if he or she is unable to speak for themselves. Respect is highly regarded, in particular when addressing or discussing an older adult. However, do not assume that because a relative calls the patient "Poppi" (or some other diminutive) that you have license to use that term. Endearing names within a family are acceptable; use of such nomenclature by a stranger is considered demeaning.

Earlier we mentioned cultural diversity within the Hispanic community. It would do well to take a little time to delve into why there are such differences. Members of each Spanish-invaded civilization largely kept their native customs and have integrated words—as well as behavior—from their ancestors into the language. So it would not be unusual to hear someone from Puerto Rico coming up with a word of Chinese origin, nor a Mexican person to do the same in Maya.

While the Spaniards may be credited with spreading the language among the civilizations they invaded, not all of their conquests gave up their own heritage. A brief history of the more common Hispanic cultures that might be encountered will demonstrate this fact.

CUBA

The first Cubans did not come from North America; they migrated from what is now Venezuela, populating the Caribbean Islands until reaching Cuba. It is estimated the first settlement occurred around 3500 B.C. Later, a group of people from what is present-day Colombia arrived; roughly speaking, the island was divided between these two groups.

In 1511 the Spaniards arrived, and so did the bloodshed and carnage. Natives were enslaved to work on the large estates carved out by the Queen of Spain. The Cubans were a proud people and many gave their lives in the cause of freedom. Some took their own lives and those of their families rather than live under the whip of despots. As a result of this and other factors, there was little intermarriage between the natives and Spaniards, leaving Cuba as one of the few Spanish-speaking civilizations with a low *mestizo* (mixed European and Native American ancestry) population.

Plantation work was grueling and many died of disease and starvation. In response, Spain imported slaves from Africa to toil in the tobacco and sugar fields. Due to the impact of slavery, about 20 percent of all Cubans today can claim African heritage. The Africans brought their culture with them, as did other groups.

MEXICO

Historians believe people came to what is now Mexico about 20,000 years ago, but the transition from hunter-gatherers to agricultural and urban living is thought to have begun with the Olmec civilization about 1200 B.C. Around 250 A.D., the Maya culture provided amazing architecture with evidence of sophisticated political and religious practices. The fourteenth century saw a rise to power of the Aztecs, who lived in the northern part of what we now call Mexico.

While the Maya declined gradually, the arrival of the Spanish conquistador, Hernán Cortés, in 1519 ravaged the Aztec civilization. Intent on securing gold and wealth by any means, Cortés and his European allies inadvertently exposed the natives to smallpox and other communicable diseases; these diseases were so devastating that the population of indigenous people dropped from around 25 million to one million.

Today there exists somewhat of an elitist culture among those of European ancestry, which is about 20 percent of the population. One can also find pockets of Mayan and Aztec towns and villages where the native dialect is spoken, not Spanish.

PUERTO RICO

In an effort to populate this island, the Spanish imported women from South America and married them. Over time, they needed additional labor for their plantations and work projects, and so the country became home to large numbers of African slaves, as well as Chinese, German, Lebanese, French, and Italian laborers. In recent years, Puerto Rico has become the refuge of immigrants from Cuba and the Dominican Republic. It is a land with a rich cultural diversity and has almost no racial discrimination. A hallmark of Puerto Rican residents is loyalty to their culture, heritage, folklore, and lifestyle.

It would be easy to go on for pages describing various Spanish-speaking countries and civilizations; the object here is to make you aware of why various groups of Hispanic people have different attitudes and ethnic differences.

ADVOCATING FOR YOUR PATIENTS

Nurses are traditionally patient advocates. With this in mind, it is helpful to consider that a patient's perception of illness and disease is crafted by their culture; it is the foundation for discernment of wellness, healing, and treatment. Culture will dictate their attitude toward the entire healthcare system, those who advocate on their behalf, and the providers of care. Whenever possible, if the medical/nursing staff can incorporate the patient's native culture into the treatment plan, then the quality of health care provided is aided tremendously.

The actions of many Hispanic patients are influenced greatly by feelings of loyalty and respect for the elder members of a family. This means that Western medical care might not be sought initially if the matriarch or patriarch of a family believes that traditional healing methods will work just as well. There are several traditional Hispanic folk remedies to be considered, some of which are specific to individual cultures. To provide quality advocacy and care, these traditions should be treated with due respect, regardless of whatever the provider's culture may be.

SOME TRADITIONAL FORMS OF HEALING

One such traditional form of healing is *curanderismo*. In Mexico, this art is conducted by a shaman or folk healer, who is usually a well-respected member of the community. *Curanderismo* is a mind-body-spirit-soul approach that works at all levels; however, it targets the soul when an individual is disabled.

Limpia is an ancient Aztec healing rite often combined with other forms of *curanderismo*. A conch shell is used as a horn to summon the spirits. The healer turns in six directions as women raise incense while turning in the same six directions representing north, south, east, west, earth, and sky. This ritual signals the start of the ancient sweat lodge, or *temazcalli*.

You might encounter patients who use and employ these and other traditional healing methods, but it is just as likely that you will have patients with no idea of these of traditional methods whatsoever. However, just because a Spanish-speaking person does not use traditional healing arts does not mean they are well versed in the current American version of healthcare. The fact is that healthcare in twenty-first century America is complex, and many people have no idea how to go about receiving the best care available to them. This is true of English-speaking people, and it is often even truer for people who are predominantly Spanish-speaking, for this latter group must navigate an intricate healthcare system in a non-native language.

VARIOUS HISPANIC ATTITUDES ABOUT HEALTH

When faced with serious illness, most Latinos will choose modern Western medicine. For ailments that are seen as minor, some Latinos may prefer traditional healing arts. If this is the case, your best stance as an advocate is to explain the benefits of Western treatment, and leave it to the doctor and patient to sort out the preferred course of action.

Some Latinos have a general attitude that emphasizes the here and now; this is a human viewpoint as old as the phrase *carpe diem* (Latin for "seize the day"). People with this attitude often believe that one's health is predetermined, or that health is a matter of luck, divine intervention, and/or powers beyond an individual's control. The challenge is to accept the patient's philosophy and work with it. At times this can be frustrating, especially when dealing with patients who have acute or chronic maladies and regard themselves as victims of malevolent spirits. You may find patients who believe they are ill by the design of God, punishment, or bad behavior. These ideas appear in many other cultures as well; the key is to remember that resistance by certain Latino patients to modern forms of treatment may be a result of such beliefs.

One way to approach patients who hold non-Western views of medicine is to build trust first. Once the patient has learned to trust you, he or she will more likely be receptive to new ideas.

HEALTH ISSUES

As an advocate for your Hispanic patients, it's important to recognize some health issues within the community:

› AIDS is four times more common in the Hispanic community as the general population.

› Gonorrhea occurs twice as often as in the general population.

› Hispanics are twice as likely to have undiagnosed type 2 diabetes as non-Hispanic Caucasians.

› Hispanics are more likely to be diagnosed with tuberculosis than Caucasians.

›

- › Breastfeeding is less common among Latinas than their non-Hispanic counterparts. Some cultures believe it is harmful to babies.

- › Many Latino men are resistant to health screening.

All these factors contribute to reduced quality healthcare. Since primary care is often delayed, the patients are much sicker when they finally present to a physician's office or emergency department. As a healthcare advocate, try to do what you can to encourage not only the patient, but also the family, and to recognize symptoms of illness that require treatment in order to prevent hospitalizations.

TERMINAL EVENT ISSUES

When the end-of-life period approaches a terminal patient, family members traditionally gather around. Women spend time caring for the individual and being stalwart; the men wander in and out of the room, but stay nearby. Nurses working in settings such as hospitals, nursing homes, hospices, and home care must be prepared to acknowledge there will be groups of visitors until the end. Many Hispanics have strong church affiliations, and such support will come in prayer meetings around the dying member.

Every person faces the end of mortal life differently; however, it is always initially sad and, while some family and friends may be quite stoic, others will engage in public displays of distress and emotion.

A FEW MORE THOUGHTS ON BEHAVIOR AND CULTURE

A proportion of Hispanic families maintain traditional gender roles. Women dictate protocol for home and children. Until they are married, girls are tightly controlled and watched closely by the men of the family. Men follow the behavioral code of *machismo*, which is to display confidence, pride, and control. These are important characteristics to consider when caring for an individual who values such traditional systems. It is not a negative and should not be viewed as such if your patient's values conflict with your own.

Family involvement is a key to success in providing patient care, no matter where you nurse. Recognize *machismo* as a fact of life. If you are a dainty female trying to get a Hispanic man to comply by being a drill sergeant, don't be too surprised if that approach doesn't work. There also may be issues if you are a male nurse caring for a woman. These concerns might not originate from the patient herself but from the dominant male in the family.

If you become aware of such a situation, utilize it to your advantage. Rather than find it an annoyance to have the family around all the time, let the family members participate in the care (without burdening them too much). Take the time to explain dietary restrictions, ambulation, and other such tasks that they can help with. Family members know more about the individual than you ever will, and they can often transform a difficult, noncompliant person into a cooperative patient.

WORKING WITH PARENTS AND FAMILIES OF SICK CHILDREN

Quite often, when a child gets sick or seriously ill, the nursing staff will be faced with the specter of the parents blaming themselves. Guilt, deserved or otherwise, can be very difficult for the people close to a patient, and it requires empathy and compassion on your part to deal with such emotions. The nurse, as a professional and trusted friend, can often be the key to changing parents' perception of the etiology of illness.

You may find that the children can speak and understand English better than their parents, and so you'll be tempted to ask your questions in English. Unless you are specifically asked to do this, however, this is not the best course of action. Doing so minimizes the role of the parent, shutting them out of the process and removing their opportunity to confirm the facts as the child has given them.

Unfortunately, access to regular healthcare is fairly low among the U.S. Hispanic population. The percentage of Hispanic adults working for employers who provide healthcare benefits is lower than the national average. In other circumstances, the high cost of health insurance sometimes makes it unaffordable. Although there is well-publicized health coverage available for the children of working poor, some Hispanics are reluctant to apply, embarrassed it will be seen as accepting welfare.

Since they do not get regular health care, Latino children have the highest rate of asthma of any ethnic group, and when they become so ill that home remedies do not work, they require hospitalization. Not surprisingly, at this stage parents are often distressed and blame themselves. Feeling guilty, parents may become quite overprotective and sometimes aggressive.

As a nurse, empathize with the parents to whatever extent is possible. Speak calmly and explain everything you are doing; ask the parent if they would like to participate in care. Acts such as these will go far in relieving the anxiety the parents feel.

There are some actions you as a nurse can take to ameliorate the situation.

› Alert Social Services. They can explain the federal program for child care, as well as put the parents in contact with organizations that offer assistance for parents of seriously ill children. This may include such financial support as utilities, transportation, food, and lodging. Some also assist with funeral expenses.

› Contact the hospital chaplain. A religious parent will welcome your intervention.

› Teach the parents about the illness. Discuss their understanding of the facts laid out by the physician-in-charge.

› Explain hospital protocol or culture. Clarify why their child is on a special diet, where to find the kitchen, and what behavior is expected of them.

› Interpret for them, if possible. This is particularly helpful when they meet with the physician.

To paraphrase an old axiom: an educated consumer makes the best patient (or family).

MAKING YOUR SPANISH-SPEAKING PATIENTS COMFORTABLE

Some people wonder whether they will be offending native Spanish-speaking individuals if they attempt to converse with them in their language, for fear of insinuating that the patient cannot speak English. Fear not: Most patients are comforted to communicate in their native language, especially when ill or out of their home environment.

Speaking of leaving the home environment: Not all nursing occurs in the hospital setting. Frequently, visiting nurses are obliged to enter the homes of patients where they will be guests. It offers a great opportunity to show you are willing to accommodate patients and family by speaking their native language. If you feel awkward, ask them if they will help you since you are learning. They won't be insulted and are likely to be happy to assist you as you serve their needs.

PATIENTS' VIEWS ABOUT YOU

In the eyes of the Hispanic culture, medical professionals generally receive a high degree of respect. The concern is whether or not practitioners are worthy of that high regard. Since many patients believe physicians do not make mistakes, they are unaware they should understand and play a role in their own health care.

It's important to initiate conversations with patients so they are at ease and will openly communicate their thoughts and concerns. Keep in mind that silence may be an indication the patient does not understand what you are saying, though they may be nodding in agreement.

Hispanics, just like everyone else, are most comfortable when they know what's going on and are partners in their own care. Very few people prefer to abdicate their control blindly. They rely on family to be around and provide support.

Here are some other general points to consider when you have a Spanish-speaking patient.

1. In some Hispanic cultures, the expression of emotion is encouraged. This means a patient may be groaning even in minor discomfort. It's not for us to judge whether they are stoic. However, you can instruct them to inform you if the pain grows worse since you may not be able to distinguish the escalation.

2. Recognize that family members prefer to provide daily care to their patients. Along those lines, male patients may become quite demanding of family in order to demonstrate they are still in control. That does not mean you have to be submissive: Such demands should apply to the family only if they elect to comply. You can be understanding without adhering. Respect is a two-way street, and you will be respected if you maintain your standards.

3. Verbal communication is important but body language can say much more. Watch for changes and observe patient reactions to understand their status and relationships with others.

4. Hispanic culture stresses friendship and respect. Once a nurse is assigned to a patient, it is in everyone's best interest to allow that relationship to grow. Some hospitals and nursing homes make a practice of rotating patients. It's something that should be avoided if possible, or the subsequent nurse should speak Spanish and establish a relationship as well.

5. Sit closer to your Hispanic patients than you might with other ethnic groups. Lean forward when speaking or listening and give them a friendly pat on the shoulder. Sitting several feet away may be perceived as being distant and uninterested.

6. Understand that the Hispanic view of medicine is occasionally a blend of traditional and folk remedies. Try to accommodate that belief if at all possible.

IN CONCLUSION

The best way to make Spanish-speaking patients and their families comfortable is to be able to communicate and not let them think they are alone. Nursing is, by nature, a caring profession; it behooves us to demonstrate that compassion to all patients regardless of the language they speak, or what other differences there might be. In times of need, nurses often must be the ones to take the first step and demonstrate our love of our brothers and sisters. That's how we make them comfortable.

AS YOU MIGHT EXPECT, it is very helpful to understand the fundamentals of Spanish before you start spouting words in that language. Learning the basic rules of Spanish should help you speak and understand spoken Spanish better, and this can only help when dealing with Spanish-speaking patients.

Fortunately, Spanish is a much more straightforward language than English. You can describe English as "complex" if you're being generous, but "tortured" works just as well. For instance, consider a word like *eight*. A person might expect this word to sound like (ee-Il-ga-hit), but in fact it's pronounced (ATE). Does that really make much sense? Continuing, you might think that by adding an *h* to the front of *eight* you would get (HATE), but no, *height* is in fact pronounced (HITE). English-speaking people take such verbal weirdness for granted after a time, but that doesn't mean it's not odd.

In contrast to English, Spanish does not have as many linguistic traps. How a word looks is typically how it's pronounced. Some letters have different pronunciations, but this and other basic points will be covered in the following section.

SPANISH ALPHABET OVERVIEW

The Spanish alphabet has 29 letters, three more than the English version. These extra letters are the consonants ch , ll, and ñ. Far from being obscure, these consonants are used in very common words by Spanish-speaking patients. For example:

Spanish Term	English Term	Spanish Example	English Example
cheque	check	*Usted puede pagar con un* **ch**eque.	You may pay with a check.
cuchillo	knife	*Se cortó el dedo con el cuchillo.*	He cut his finger with the knife.
pe**ch**o	chest	*El paciente tiene dolor en el pe**ch**o.*	The patient has chest pain.
llorar	to cry	*La niña no para de **ll**orar.*	The girl does not stop crying.
tobi**ll**o	ankle	*Juan tiene dolor en el tobi**ll**o.*	John has ankle pain.
rodi**ll**a	knee	*El tiene una rodi**ll**a fracturada.*	He has a fractured knee.
a**ñ**o	year	*Tomás fue hospitalizado el a**ñ**o pasado.*	Thomas was hospitalized last year.
mu**ñ**eca	wrist	*El paciente tiene una mu**ñ**eca torcida.*	The patient has a sprained wrist.

Some people will say that the Spanish alphabet actually has 30 letters. This is a common error based on the confusion with the digraph "rr," or "double r." This digraph sounds like the "r" in English, but with more strength. One basic rule for the double "r" is that no Spanish words begin with it. Here are some examples that will help you get familiar with "rr."

Spanish Term	English Term	Spanish Example	English Example
hemorragia	hemorrhage	*La paciente tuvo una hemorragia.*	The patient had a hemorrhage.
hemorroide	hemorrhoid	*El doctor dijo que necesito tratamiento para las hemorroides.*	The doctor said I need treatment for hemorrhoids.

Here are some words that begin with each letter in the Spanish alphabet. When possible, we used terms you might need when speaking Spanish to a patient.

SPANISH VOWELS:

A: *agua*/water
E: *emergencia*/emergency
I: *inmune*/immune
O: *ojos*/eyes
U: *uña*/fingernail

SPANISH CONSONANTS:	**L:** *laringe*/larynx	**V:** *venas*/veins
B: *boca*/mouth	**LL:** *llorar*/to cry	**W:** *waterpolo*/waterpolo
C: *cuello*/neck	**M:** *manos*/hands	**X:** *examen*/test
Ch: *pecho*/chest	**N:** *nariz*/nose	**Y:** *yodo*/iodine
D: *dedos*/fingers	**Ñ:** *cañón*/canyon	**Z:** *zapatos*/shoes
F: *feto*/fetus	**P:** *pulmones*/lungs	
G: *garganta*/throat	**Q:** *quebrado*/broken	
H: *hospital*/hospital	**R:** *riñones*/ kidneys	
J: *jefe*/boss	**S:** *sudar*/to sweat	
K: *kilo*/kilo	**T:** *tobillo*/ankle	

The Spanish alphabet is composed of the same five vowels as the English alphabet. More importantly, Spanish vowels are always the same, spoken or written. This is one of the main reasons that Spanish words are spelled exactly as they sound.

Speaking of sound, the table on the following pages covers how each Spanish letter sounds. As in the previous list, we used medical words when possible.

Spanish Alphabet	English Example	Spanish Example	🎧	Pronounciation Rules and Tips
A	mama father	*año* (year) *amígdalas* (tonsils)		**A** is pronounced like the "a" in "father" or "astonish" and like the "o" in "hop."
B	**b**at **b**orrow	*boca* (mouth) *brazo* (arm)		**B** sounds like the "b" in "borrow."
C	before a, o, u: **c**at, **c**ut before e, i: **c**ity, **c**ell	*cabeza* (head) *ceja* (eyebrow)		**C** before the vowels "a," "o," or "u" (ca, co, cu) is pronounced as "k" in "kilo." Before "e" and "i" (ce, ci), it sounds like "c" in" ceiling" or "s" in "sailor."
CH	**ch**air	*cheque* (check) *chico* (small)		**Ch** has a similar sound as the same English construction "ch" in "chair" and "chalk."
D	**d**o, **D**avid	*dolor* (pain) *codo* (elbow)		**D** has two different sounds, hard and soft: When "d" begins a word (and after the letter "n" or "i"), the hard Spanish "d" is pronounced like the "d" in the word "dog." One difference is that when pronouncing the hard Spanish "d," the tongue touches the back of the front teeth. When "d" is located between vowels, it is pronounced more softly, like the "th" sound in the word "this."

Spanish Alphabet	English Example	Spanish Example	🎧	Pronounciation Rules and Tips
E	ten, desk	*estómago* (stomach) *espinilla* (shin)		**E** is often pronounced as the "a" in the word "date," but shorter. **E** also produces the "ay" sound in "pay." This vowel is never silent as it is in English words ending in "e," such as "cake" or "debate."
F	fire, **ph**oto	*fiebre* (fever) *frente* (forehead)		**F** sounds like "f" in "fire" and also like "f" in "front" or "ph" in "philosophy."
G	gallon, gala	*garganta* (throat) *glúteos* (gluteus)		**G** is pronounced in three separate sounds: hard, soft, and an "h" sound. **G** before "a," "o," and "u" sounds like "g" in "gall" or "w" in "war." This is the hard "g" sound. The soft "g" sound is not like any English sound, and it is not easy for English-only speakers to pronounce without some practice. This sound occurs mostly between vowels like *agua* (water) and *aguacate* (avocado). When **g** comes before "e" or "i," it sounds like the "h" in the words "hot" or "hotel."
H	**h**our, **h**onest	*huesos* (bones) *hemorragia* (hemorrhage)		**H** in Spanish is always mute; it has no sound at all. This means "huesos" has to be read as "uesos" and never as "juesos."

Spanish Alphabet	English Example	Spanish Example	🎧	Pronounciation Rules and Tips
I	see	*irritación* (irritation) *infección* (infection)		**I** is pronounced as "ee" in the word "see," except that the sound is shorter.
J	hot, hat	*ojos* (eyes) *joven* (young person)		**J** has the same sound as the "h" in "hotel "and "heart."
K	kilogram, Kathy	*kilogramo* (kilogram) *kilo* (kilo)		**K** is only used in words borrowed from other languages, such as "kilo." The K has the same sound as it does in English words like "Kentucky."
L	lake, liver	*laringe* (larynx) *lengua* (tongue)		**L** has a similar sound in both English and Spanish.
LL	million, billion	*llorar* (to cry) *lleno* (full)		**LL** is a double consonant that sounds like "y" in "yes" or like the "lli" in the word "million."
M	mammography, molar	*mamografía* (mammography) *muelas* (molars)		**M** has the same sound as in English.

Spanish Alphabet	English Example	Spanish Example	🎧	Pronunciation Rules and Tips
N	**n**erves, **n**utritional	*n*utritivo (nutritive) *n*ervios (nerves)		**N** sounds the same as in English.
Ñ	ca**ny**on	ni*ñ*a (girl) a*ñ*o (year)		**Ñ** is a bit of a tricky consonant. It has a unique sound that it can be related to the sound of "niy-" followed by a vowel, and it also sounds like the "ny" in the word "canyon."
O	n**o**, **o**rthopedic	*ó*rgano (organ) *o*reja (ear)		**O** is pronounced like the "o" in the word "no," but shorter.
P	**p**otato, s**p**ot	*p*ulmones (lungs) *p*ediatra (pediatrician)		**P** has the same sound as it does in English words like "potato" or "park."
Q	**k**id, **k**itten	*q*uemadura (burn) *q*uebrado (broken)		**Q** always appears in combination with the letter "u" followed by either an "i" or an "e." Q is pronounced like the "k" in the word "kit."

Spanish Alphabet	English Example	Spanish Example	🎧 Pronounciation Rules and Tips
R	red, river	*corazón* (heart) *radiografía* (x-ray)	**R** has the same basic sound as the "r" in English, but the duration of the sound is shorter. When two r's are placed together, you get the same "r" sound as in English, but there's more strength. (The two rr's can also be described as a trill.)
S	said, spinal	*sudar* (to sweat) *senos* (chest)	**S** has the same English sound as in "salt" or "said."
T	tetanus, tomatoes	*tos* (cough) *tuberculosis* (tuberculosis)	**T** sounds always like the "t" in "time" and "taste."
U	due, flute	*útero* (utero) *úlcera* (ulcer)	**U** is usually pronounced like the "oo" in "broom" or the "u" in "flute." Never pronounce the Spanish "u" like the "u" in "universe." In addition, the Spanish "u" becomes a silent vowel when following "q" (as in *queso* or *que*) or when it is used in the "gui" or "gue" combination (as in *guerra*, *guitarra*, or *guerrero*).
V	boy, baby	*vacuna* (vaccine) *venas* (veins)	The Spanish **B**—called long b (*be larga*)—and **V**—called short b (*be corta*)—are pronounced the same.

Spanish Alphabet	English Example	Spanish Example	🎧	Pronounciation Rules and Tips
W	**w**ater, **w**indy	*Wilfredo* (a Spanish name)		**W** is only used in words borrowed from other languages such as "waterpolo" or "Wendira" (a female Hispanic name).
X	tal**ks**	e**x**amen (exam) Mé**x**ico (Mexico)		The consonant **X** has three separate sounds. **X** is pronounced as "ks" in the word "talks" (*examen*). **X** is pronounced as the English letter "h" and is reserved for certain proper nouns and words that are derived from them (*México, mexicano*). **X** is pronounced like the English "ch" and is reserved for certain proper nouns (*Xitle, Xela*).
Y	**y**es, **j**oy	*yo* (I) *mayor* (older)		A special case, **Y** acts as both a consonant and as a vowel. As a consonant, y has two common sounds. The first sounds like the English "y" in the word "yes" or the "j" in the English word "joy." As a vowel, y sounds like "ee" in the word "beep." An example is *rey* (king).
Z	**th**ink, **th**eft, **s**ay	*zapato* (shoe) *corazón* (heart)		The Spanish **Z** is pronounced differently in Spain than in Latin America. In Spain, it is pronounced like the "th" in the English word "think." In Latin America, it is pronounced like the letter "s" as in "salt."

IMPORTANT CONSONANT RULES

The following list provides some information about how Spanish consonants differ from their English counterparts.

› Except for h, there are no mute letters like "b" in "lamb" or "n" in "autumn."

› In Spanish, consonants are rarely doubled. In English, consonants like "f", "s", and "t" are often doubled in words like "offer," "confess," and "letter."

› The only consonants that will be doubled in Spanish are "c" and "n." "C" is found doubled in words like *accidente* (accident). "N" is found doubled in words having the prefix "in" and elsewhere; examples are *innato* (innate) and *perenne* (perennial). There are not too many of these exceptions in the common Spanish vocabulary.

› The Spanish consonants v, ll, h, j, r, z, and x have different pronunciation in English.

› The consonant "ñ" does not exist in English, but you can pronounce it as the sound of "ny" as in "canyon."

PRACTICE MAKES PERFECT

Ideally, you can practice your pronunciation of Spanish with someone who is familiar with the language already. If they can understand you, then you've said it correctly! However, even if you only practice with a cat or a plant, it's still very helpful to start training your mouth to speak Spanish, your ear to hear Spanish, and your brain to process Spanish words and sentences.

Vowels	Consonants	Spanish Example	English Example
a, e, i, o	d, l, g, n, m, s, t	*Ana tiene dolor de estómago.*	Ana has stomach pain.
e, o	**ch** (pronounced as "ch" in church, Charlie), **d, g, l, n, p, t**	*Tengo dolor en el pecho.*	I have chest pain.
a, e, i, o	**b, c, f, ll** (is pronounced as "j" in Jack, joke), **m, n, p, r**	*¡Mi bebé no para de lorar! Creo que tiene fiebre.*	My baby doesn't stop crying! I think he has a fever.
a, e, i, o, u	**c, d, m, n, ñ, o, p, x**	*Usted necesita un examen de mamografía cada año.*	You need a breast exam every year.
a, e, i, o	**d, l, m, n, s, t**	*El niño está vomitando.*	The boy is vomiting.

WHERE TO STRESS OR EMPHASIZE SPANISH WORDS

As in the English language, placing the stress in a word properly makes the difference between good and poor pronunciation. Here are some basic rules regarding where to stress or emphasize Spanish words.

› Words in singular and in plural keep the same stress on the same syllable.

*en**fer**mo/en**fer**mos* (sick)
*medi**ci**na/medi**ci**nas* (medicine/medicines)
***ma**no/**ma**nos* (hand/hands)

› If a word ends in the consonants **d**, **r**, **l**, or **z**, the stress falls on the last syllable.

cavidad (cavity), *ansiedad* (anxiety)

*La mujer tuvo un ataque de ansie**dad**./*
The woman had an anxiety attack.

› If a word ends in a vowel (**a**, **e**, **i**, **o**, **u**), or in the consonants **n** or **s**, the stress falls on the next-to-last syllable.

cama (bed) *dedos* (fingers)
*Usted necesita permanecer en **ca**ma por una semana.*
You need to stay in bed for one week.

Spanish words do not always follow these rules. Fortunately, Spanish often provides you with a visual marker that tells you which syllable needs to be stressed. This is presented by placing an acute accent mark (´) over a letter in the syllable to be stressed. How convenient is that?

The acute accent is always over a vowel in the stressed syllable in a word.

*El paciente tiene problemas del cora**zón**.*
The patient has heart problems.

In this case, the emphasis in this example is the last syllable: co/ra/**zón**

*El doctor me dijo que tengo una infec-ción en mi ri**ñón** izquierdo.*
The doctor said I have an infection in my left kidney.

Here, the emphasis is the last syllables: in/fec/**ción** and ri/**ñón**

Another important attribute of the acute accent (sometimes called the "graphic accent") is the differentiation it makes in words that are spelled the same but have a different meaning.

Be sure to keep this in mind, as no father likes to be called a spud.

mamá (mother)	*mama* (breast)
él (he)	*el* (the)
papá (father)	*papa* (potato)

When an acute accent appears over the vowels "u" and "i," it causes them to be pronounced apart from the vowel near them. This breaks the dipthong or semi-consonant.

cirugía/surgery (si-roo-HEE-ah)
pulmonía/pulmonary (pool-mo-NEE-ah)
aún/still (ah-OON)

Every question word in Spanish has an accent mark.

¿Dónde? (Where?) *¿Cuándo?* (When?)
¿Qué? (What?) *¿Quién?* (Who?)

¿Cómo? (How?)   ¿Cuál? (Which)
¿Por qué? (Why?)   ¿Cuánto? (How much?)

In addition, questions in Spanish are indicated by an inverted question mark at the beginning of the sentence and a normal question mark at the end. Declarative sentences will have an inverted exclamation point at the beginning and a normal exclamation point at the end.

In general, the acute accent is used when the stress falls in a "non-normal" place in a word. The accent on the vowels á, é, í, ó, ú is used to indicate that stress falls on those syllables in cases where these rules do not apply.

maní (peanut)
subí (I climbed)
comí (I ate)

UNDERSTANDING SPANISH-SPEAKING PATIENTS

America and England were once described as "two nations divided by a common language." In other words, what counts as English (in pronunciation and spelling) is not always the same depending on where you are in the world and who is doing the speaking. This same distinction also holds true for Spanish. Although there is a great deal of similarity, there are also differences in the pronunciation of Spanish between people from Spain and those from Latin America. For instance, the sound of the consonants B, C, V, W, and Z are much stronger in the Spanish from Spain than they are in the Spanish from Latin America. While such variations in dialects can be confusing, speaking clearly and carefully will always help, and simply knowing that people might say the word slightly differently should also be beneficial.

As we mentioned earlier, words in Spanish are usually pronounced just as they are written, a fact that makes pronunciation easier. This same fact often makes native Spanish speakers pronounce every letter in an English word, but since English has all sorts of mystifying rules and conventions, this doesn't always work very well. Consider a word like *thought*, and you can see the problems that might arise.

When you are speaking Spanish, keep these guidelines in mind:

> Don't worry about speaking with a Spanish accent. Most Spanish speakers will be able to understand you if you just speak slowly and clearly.

> Pronouncing words correctly is more important than talking quickly. When you become more fluent you can increase your speed.

> When communicating with a Spanish-speaking patient, you might think they are talking too fast for you to understand. One possible reason for this is that the sound of the vowels in Spanish is shorter than in English. Your ear, accustomed to English, perceives this as if the vowel sounds are getting cut off, but in fact, that's how they are spoken. To remedy this, just ask the speaker to repeat the sentences, slowly.

- yes: Spanish-speaking students will pronounce "yes" as "sseee," while native Spanish speakers will pronounce "se-."

- no: Spanish-speaking students will pronounce "no" as "nnooo," while native Spanish speakers will pronounce "no-."

› Practice, practice, and practice. It's what is needed to open your ear to the Spanish language. Don't be shy if you are not fluent. Your patients will greatly appreciate the fact that you're trying to learn their language in order to understand their health concerns better.

› In Hispanic culture, the ability to speak more than one language is considered a sign of culture and intelligence. Many patients will feel more confident and more familiar with you if you show you are able to grasp some basic Spanish.

SPANISH VERBS AND PRONOUNS

Remember how we said that Spanish was less complex than English? That's still mostly true, but when it comes to conjugating verbs, Spanish is a bit trickier than English. That doesn't mean you can skip learning about it completely, though. This section will provide you with the necessary basic skills, but in no way is it a comprehensive discussion of the subject.

First, though, let's go back to grade school and review the basics of conjugating English verbs. Present, past, and future are the three basic tenses for verb conjugation. Additionally, recall that there are two kinds of verbs in English: (1) regular verbs, those ones that change to the past tense using the suffix "ed," and (2) irregular verbs, where the past tense form is different in each case.

Now that you remember your basic English grammar, we can start with some basic Spanish. Spanish verb construction contains 11 different tenses (time and mood). In addition, in Spanish the regular and irregular verbs do not follow the same rules as in English. Each verb has a different way to be conjugated. The following table is an example, showing verb tense in both English and Spanish side by side.

WHERE IS "IT"?

As you may have noticed, the English pronoun "it" doesn't really have a Spanish counterpart. This is because most objects are attributed either masculine or feminine properties. This doesn't mean they are male or female; it just means that masculine or feminine pronouns and other masculine/feminine language rules apply to them. This is another tricky area of Spanish that can be glossed over for now; if you want to learn to speak Spanish fluently, you'll have to learn more in this area, but for now, just understand for certain that there are more masculine/feminine language differences in Spanish than there are in English.

As you'll see, there are two variations in the English conjugation and six in the Spanish. Before panicking, let us start with the three basic tenses: present, past, and future. It will help to understand how verbs in Spanish are divided.

English Pronoun	English Verb	Spanish Pronoun	Spanish Verb
I	eat	Yo	como
You	eat	Tú	comes
It	eats		come
He	eats	Él	come
She	eats	Ella	come
We	eat	Nosotros/Nosotras	comemos
You	eat	Vosotros/Vosotras	coméis
They	eat	Ellos/Ellas	comen

VERB CATEGORIES

Spanish verbs are the "Achilles heel" of Spanish grammar. Conjugating becomes very complex because of its different tenses, combinations, and moods. You can find up to 50 conjugated forms per verb, but heed our advice and don't go looking for all 50 unless you want to learn to speak Spanish fluently.

Some good news: Verbs that end in -ar, -er, and -ir are conjugated in the same way in all the tenses. If you learn how to conjugate one regular verb in each category, you will be able to conjugate the rest.

	hablar/to talk	*amar*/to love	*visitar*/to visit
Yo	hablo	amo	visito
Tú	hablas	amas	visitas
Él	habla	ama	visita
Ella	habla	ama	visita
Nosotros/Nosotras	hablamos	amamos	visitamos
Vosotros/Vosotras	habláis	amáis	visitáis
Ellos/Ellas	hablan	aman	visitan
	atender/to care for	*entender*/to understand	*hacer*/to do
Yo	atiendo	entiendo	hago
Tú	atiendes	entiendes	haces
Él	atiende	entiende	hace
Ella	atiende	entiende	hace
Nosotros/Nosotras	atienden	entendemos	hacemos
Vosotros/Vosotras	atendéis	entendéis	hacéis
Ellos/Ellas	atienden	entienden	hacen

	escribir/to write	*vivir*/to live	*subir*/to climb
Yo	escribo	vivo	subo
Tú	escribes	vives	subes
Él	escribe	vive	sube
Ella	escribe	vive	sube
Nosotros/Nosotras	escribimos	vivimos	subimos
Vosotros/Vosotras	escribís	vivís	subís
Ellos/Ellas	escriben	viven	suben

Those are the simple verbs; if you run across one of them, rejoice. In contrast, irregular verbs have unique, irregular conjugations, and the only way to learn them is through memorization. The verb *ir* is one of the most common irregular verbs.

Example: *ir*/to go

English Pronoun	Spanish Pronoun	Spanish Verb Conjugation
I	*Yo*	voy
You	*Tú*	vas
He	*Él*	va
She	*Ella*	va
We	*Nosotros/Nosotras*	vamos
You	*Vosotros/Vosotras*	vais
They	*Ellos/Ellas*	van

Keep in mind that you already know many, many irregular verbs, since many English verbs—

such as "to go"—also have irregular conjugations. If you can learn them in English, you can learn them in Spanish as well.

Spanish verbs are conjugated in four categories known as **moods**. These moods are the indicative, subjunctive, imperative, and non-personal moods. If this were a Spanish class, we would cover all of these moods, but since we're here to give you the basics, this section will focus only on the indicative mood, which includes the present, imperfect, preterite (a past tense), and future tenses.

The indicative present tense is a good place to start. It is used quite often in Spanish communication, and it functions very similarly to the English present tense. Start practicing the present tense with these examples.

		trabajar/ to work	*estudiar/to study*	*beber/to drink*
I	Yo	trabajo	estudio	bebo
You	Tú	trabajas	estudias	bebes
He	Él	trabaja	estudia	bebe
She	Ella	trabaja	estudia	bebe
We	Nosotros/Nosotras	trabajamos	estudiamos	bebemos
You	Vosotros/Vosotras	trabajáis	estudiáis	bebéis
They	Ellos/Ellas	trabajan	estudian	beben

Note that there is more than one way to translate *el trabaja* from Spanish to English. This could mean "He works," but it could also be translated as "He is working" or "He does work."

For the future tense, things get a bit trickier. Fortunately, the future tense conjugations are typically the same for verbs ending in *-ar*, *-er*, and *-ir*.

		trabajar/to work	*estudiar*/to study	*beber*/to drink
I	*Yo*	*trabajaré*	*estudiaré*	*beberé*
You	*Tú*	*trabajarás*	*estudiarás*	*beberás*
He	*Él*	*trabajará*	*estudiará*	*beberá*
She	*Ella*	*trabajará*	*estudiará*	*beberá*
We	*Nosotros/Nosotras*	*trabajaremos*	*estudiaremos*	*beberemos*
You	*Vosotros/Vosotras*	*trabajaréis*	*estudiaréis*	*beberéis*
They	*Ellos/Ellas*	*trabajarán*	*estudiarán*	*beberán*

Spanish has two simple past tenses: the preterite (or preterit) and the imperfect. The preterite is used to refer to a completed action in a sentence. In other words, if the verb refers to an action that has a clear end, then the preterite is used. The preterite is used to communicate:

1. An action that happened once.

   Yo fui ayer al doctor.   I went to the doctor yesterday.

   Hablé con la enfermera.   I spoke with the nurse.

2. An action that happened more than once but with a specific end.

   Yo fui ayer al doctor dos veces.   I went to the doctor two times yesterday.

   Hablé con la enfermera dos veces.   I spoke with the nurse two times.

3. The beginning or end of a determinate process.

| *El se enfermó.* | He got sick. |
| *La reunión se terminó a las 3 P.M.* | The meeting ended at 3 P.M. |

Also known as the "incomplete," the imperfect indicative is used to refer to an action that doesn't have a specific ending. In the English language, a simple past tense in a sentence such as "he ran" can be converted into Spanish by using either the preterite (*corrió*) or the imperfect indicative (*corría*). The imperfect indicative is used to communicate:

1. The habitual past or repeated actions.

Iba al doctor.	I used to go to the doctor.
Hablábamos con la enfermera.	We would speak with the nurse.
Los niños se lavaban las manos.	The children would wash their hands.

2. To describe an action that occurred over an unspecified time.

| *Los pacientes se lavaban las manos.* | The patients were washing their hands. |
| *Mientras el doctor examinaba al paciente, la enfermera escribía.* | While the doctor examined the patient, the nurse was writing. |

3. To describe a circumstance or situation from the past.

| *Juan quería estar sano.* | John wanted to be healthy. |
| *El niño tenía fiebre.* | The boy had a fever. |

4. To indicate time or age in the past.

Era la una de la mañana.   It was one o'clock in the morning.
La mujer enferma tenía 60 años.   The sick woman was 60 years old.

Take a look at three simple tenses in both languages.

Spanish Pronouns	English Noun	English Present Tense	Spanish Present Tense	English Past Tense	Spanish Past Tense	English Future Tense	Spanish Future Tense
Yo	I	study	estudio	studied	estudiaba / estudié	will study	estudiaré
Tú	you		estudias		estudiabas / estudiaste		estudiarás
Él/Ella	it/he/she	studies	estudia		estudiaba / estudió		estudiará
Nosotras/os	we	study	estudiamos		estudiábamos / -amos		estudiaremos
Vosotras/os	you		estudiáis		estudiabais / -asteis		estudiaréis
Ellas/os	they		estudian		estudiaban / -aron		estudiarán

As you can see, conjugating verbs in Spanish is not something you learn in a day or two. That's okay. Even if you don't pick up every conjugation of a verb, there is still a good chance a patient will understand what you're saying if you are somewhat close to the proper verb form. Look at the previous chart; everything starts with *estudi-*, so if you get that part of the verb right, you stand a good chance of being understood.

NUMBER AND PERSON OF VERBS

The number value of the verb is determined by the subject. It can be singular or plural, just like in English.

| singular | I speak. | *Yo hablo.* |
| plural | We speak. | *Nosotros hablamos.* |

The person categories are first, second, and third person singular, and first, second, and third person plural.

first person singular	I eat.	*Yo como.*
second person singular	You eat.	*Tú comes.*
third person singular	He (She) eats.	*Él (Ella) come.*
first person plural	We eat.	*Nosotros (Nosotras) comemos.*
second person plural	You eat.	*Vosotros (Vosotras) coméis.*
third person plural	They eat.	*Ellos comen.*
second person plural (formal)	You eat.	*Ustedes comen.*

In this chart, you can see that the second

person pronoun (you) is the same in English for both singular and plural, but different in Spanish (*tú, vosotros,* or *vosotras*). In Spanish (and other Latin-based languages), the singular form is more familiar, while the plural form is more formal. Since you probably want to be more formal with patients, stick to the second person plural form when you can. And while we're on the subject of which pronoun to use…

SPANISH PRONOUNS

There are five types of common and widely used pronouns, and each will be discussed briefly.

PRONOUN #1: SUBJECT PRONOUNS

Subject pronouns take the place of the subject or the person who performed the action in a sentence. The subject pronoun is often avoided when the verb forms make the sentence clear enough. When that is the case, the pronouns shouldn't be used.

Yo	I
Tú	You
Él, Ella, Usted	He/She/ You
N/A	It
Nosotros	We
Vosotros	You (familiar)
Ellos/Ellas, Ustedes	They, You (formal)

Example: *El Doctor Rodríguez y la Doctora Perez son excelentes profesionales. Él es cirujano y ella es ginecóloga. Quieren abrir su propia clínica pronto.*

Doctor Rodriguez and Doctor Perez are excellent professionals. He is a surgeon and she is a gynecologist. They would like to open their own clinic soon.

Note that in the third sentence (*Quieren abrir su propia clínica pronto.*), it is not necessary to use the pronoun. The meaning remains clear.

PRONOUN #2: DIRECT OBJECT PRONOUNS

Direct object pronouns replace the person or thing to which the action is done directly. Direct objects are the same in Spanish and English. For example, if a patient loses a prescription, the patient is the subject, the verb is lost, and the direct object is the prescription.

El paciente perdió la receta./The patient lost the prescription.
What did the patient lose? *La receta*/the prescription.

Looking at the chart, you can see that the order of the words is different in Spanish than it is in English. In English, the direct object follows the verb, while in Spanish it precedes it. We'll discuss the sequence of words in a sentence more thoroughly later in this chapter.

English Direct Object Pronoun	Spanish Direct Object Pronoun	English Example	Spanish Example
Me	Me	He loves me.	Él me ama.
You (familiar)	Te	John loves you.	Juan te ama.
Him, her, it, you (formal)	Lo (masculine) / La (feminine)	She loves him.	Ella lo ama.
Us	Nos	She loves us.	Ella nos ama.
You (familiar plural)	Os		Ella os ama.
Them, you (plural formal)	Los (masculine) / Las (feminine)	She loves them.	Ella los ama.

PRONOUN #3: INDIRECT OBJECT PRONOUNS

Indirect object pronouns represent a person or a thing that is affected by the action done to something or someone else. The indirect object pronoun must appear regardless of whether the noun is present in the sentence.

Example:

El doctor le recetó píldoras a Rosario.   The doctor prescribed pills to Rosario.

What did the doctor prescribe? Pills! In this example, pills are the indirect object(s.) They are the thing that actually receives the action; Rosario is the person who is affected by the action. Some verbs almost always have an indirect object:

Vender/to sell	*Dar*/to give	*Pasar*/to pass	*Prometer*/to promise
Contar/to count	*Decir*/to say	*Mentir*/to lie	*Explicar*/to explain

English Pronouns	Spanish Indirect Object Pronouns	English Example	Spanish Example
Me	Me	The doctor gave me the medicine.	*El doctor me dió la medicina.*
You (familiar)	Te	The doctor gave you the medicine.	*El doctor te dió la medicina.*
Him, her, it, you (formal)	Le	The doctor gave her the medicine.	*El doctor le dió la medicina.*
Us	Nos	The doctor gave us the medicine.	*El doctor nos dió la medicina.*
You (familiar plural)	Os	The doctor gave you the medicine.	*El doctor os dió la medicina.*
Them, you (plural formal)	Les	The doctor gave them the medicine.	*El doctor les dió la medicina.*

PRONOUN #4: OBJECT OF A PREPOSITION PRONOUNS

Just like its name suggests, this covers the pronoun immediately following a preposition.

Yo traigo dos vestidos, uno para mí y otro para Griselda.

I have two dresses, one for me and another for Griselda.

In this example the "*mí*" (me) is the pronoun following the preposition *para* (for).

English Pronouns	Object of a Preposition Pronouns	English Example	Spanish Example
Me	*Mí*	It is a lunch for me.	*Es un almuerzo para mí.*
You (familiar)	*Ti*	It is a lunch for you.	*Es un almuerzo para ti.*
Him, her, it, you (formal)	*Él, ella, usted*	It is a lunch for her.	*Es un almuerzo para ella.*
Us	*Nosotros*	It is a lunch for us.	*Es un almuerzo para nosotros.*
You (familiar plural)	*Vosotros*	It is a lunch for you.	*Es un almuerzo para vosotros.*
Them, you (plural formal)	*Ellos, ellas, ustedes*	It is a lunch for them.	*Es un almuerzo para ellos.*

PRONOUN #5: REFLEXIVE PRONOUNS

Reflexive pronouns are preceded by a noun to which they refer. In English, the reflexive pronouns end in *-self* or *-selves*.

Example:

Mateo se pregunta si él podría ser exitoso./Matthew asked himself if he can be successful.

In this sentence, Mateo (the subject) asks himself (*se*, the reflexive pronoun). The following chart summarizes all of the Spanish pronouns.

Subject		Direct Object		Indirect Object		Object of Preposition		Reflexive	
Yo	Nosotros	Me	Nos	Me	Nos	Mí	Nosotros	Me	Nos
Tú	Vosotros	Te	Os	Te	Os	Ti	Vosotros	Te	Os
Él, ella, usted	Ellos/as, ustedes	Lo, la	Los, las	Le	Les	Él, ella, usted	Ellos/as, ustedes	Se	Se

Again, it bears repeating that learning Spanish verb conjugation and memorizing every Spanish pronoun are two tasks that take some time to accomplish, and you don't actually need to do either of them to use the phrases in this book effectively. Whatever you learn about Spanish will help you with the phrases, and if you continue to speak Spanish on a regular basis, you should gain a better understanding of the language as you go along. For now, just keep in mind that there are many, many conjugation rules, and that pronouns can be a little tricky. That basic understanding is all you need when you are first starting out.

BASIC SPANISH WORD ORDER

Once again, we return to an area where Spanish trumps English. When it comes to word order in a sentence, Spanish has greater flexibility, and this added flexibility should help your patients understand you better (and vice versa). You see, English speakers always tend to follow the common English word order of (subject+verb+object). That's fine, but with Spanish, this order can vary and still be correct. Frequently used statements can start with the verb, the subject, or the object, and the sentence retains its meaning.

Variation in the Spanish Word Order			English Common Word Order
Subject + Verb + Object	Verb + Object + Subject	Object + Verb + Subject	Subject + Verb + Object
La bebé toma leche.	*Toma leche la bebé.*	*Leche toma la bebé.*	*The baby drinks milk.*

All of the sentences are correct in Spanish. What this means to you is that if you know the Spanish words for "doctor," "give, " and "injection," you can relay the concept "The doctor will give you an injection" just by stringing those words together in some order. Your sentence might not be pretty, but it should be understood.

Here you can see the word order in this simple example can vary and the meaning of the sentence is not lost: "The baby drinks milk." For English speakers it can look like the sentence is out of order, but that is just how flexible the Spanish language is.

The following chart gives you examples of the different kinds of word order you can use in Spanish. The big idea to take away is that word order for Spanish sentences is not as strict as it is in English.

Type of Sentence	Word Order	Example in Spanish	Example Translated into English
Statement	Subject + verb	*El niño llora.*	*The boy cries.*
Statement	Subject + verb + object	*La enfermera inyectó al paciente.*	*The nurse injected the patient.*
Statement	Subject + object pronoun + verb	*El doctor lo recetó.*	*The doctor prescribed it.*
Statement	Verb + subject	*Vomitó la mujer.*	*The woman vomited.*
Statement	Object + verb + subject	*La medicina fue recetado por el doctor.*	*The doctor prescribed the medicine.*
Statement	Adverb + verb + subject	*Siempre lloran los bebés.*	*The babies always cry.*
Question	Question + verb + subject	*¿Dónde están las recetas?*	*Where are the prescriptions?*
Question	Question word + verb + subject	*¿Dónde está el laboratorio?*	*Where is the laboratory?*
Exclamation	Exclamatory word + adjective + verb + subject	*¡Que buena es la enfermera!*	*The nurse is very nice!*
Phrase	Noun + adjective	*La clínica cerca*	*The nearby clinic*
Phrase	Adjective + noun	*Otras enfermedades*	*Other diseases*

Type of Sentence	Word Order	Example in Spanish	Example Translated into English
Phrase	Preposition + noun	*En la clínica*	*In the clinic*
Command	Verb + subject pronoun	*Respire usted*	*You breathe*
Command	Verb + noun	*Abra la boca.*	*Open your mouth.*

As shown earlier, another point about Spanish word order is that when the subject is obvious and understood in the first sentence, it can be omitted in the following sentences.

Ana *tiene una cita médica* (Ana has an appointment). *Tiene una cita médica.*
In the second sentence, the subject (Ana) is omitted.

LIST OF SPANISH WORDS AND PHRASES

That concludes our whirlwind tour of basic Spanish grammar. The rest of the chapter is devoted to common Spanish words and phrases; learning these will help you speak Spanish in general, if that is something you would like to do.

These words and phrases are frequently used in any kind of communication in Spanish. When possible, we have grouped the words by topic.

Spanish Common Words	English Translation	Spanish Common Words	English Translation
hola	hi	*con*	with
yo	I	*aquí*	here
tú/usted	you (informal)/ you (formal)	*allí*	there
él	he	*hoy*	today
ella	she	*mañana*	tomorrow
nosotros/vosotros	us/us for Argentina, Colombia, and Spain	*un/una*	a
sí	yes	*quizás*	maybe
no	no	*hombre*	man
el/la	the	*mujer*	woman
y	and	*niño*	boy
o	or	*niña*	girl

Spanish Common Words	English Translation	Spanish Common Words	English Translation
pero	but	padre	father
en	in	madre	mother
de	of	hijo	son
por	for	hija	daughter
hermano	brother	día	day
hermana	sister	noche	night
marido	husband	grande	big
esposa/esposas	wife/handcuffs	pequeño	small
agua	water	bueno	good
carro	car	malo	bad
ropa	clothes	feliz	happy
nombre	name	triste	sad
casa	house	ahora	now
tienda	store	nunca	never
teléfono	telephone	siempre	always

Spanish Common Words	English Translation	Spanish Common Words	English Translation
televisión	television	*amor*	love
persona	person	*odio*	hate
muy	very	*poco*	little
mucho	much		

SPANISH COGNATES

There is a small but important number of words that are identical in spelling and meaning in both languages. These words are called **cognates**. Learning these should be easy, shouldn't it?

actor	altar	angular	animal	banana	chocolate	terrible
color	cruel	horrible	hospital	hotel	metal	tropical
motor	natural	opinion	radio	sofa	taxi	no

SPANISH COMMON PHRASES

These are simple phrases everyone should learn if they travel to a Spanish-speaking country, because all across the world, people don't mind if foreigners can't speak their language as long as they're polite about it.

Spanish Popular Phrases	English Translation
🎧 SALUTATION	
¡Hola!	Hi!
¡Buenos días!	Good morning!
¡Buenas tardes!	Good evening!
¡Buenas noches!	Good night!
¡Bienvenido!/¡Bienvenidos!	Welcome!
¿Cómo está usted?	How are you?
¡Estoy bien, gracias! ¿Y usted?	I'm fine, thanks, and you?
¡Muy bien!	Very good!
¡Más o menos!	So-so!

Spanish Popular Phrases	English Translation
¡Muchas gracias!	Thank you very much!
¡De nada!	Don't mention it!
¡Un placer!	My pleasure!
¡Hasta luego!	See you later!
¿Qué hay de nuevo?	What is new?
¡Adios!	Goodbye!
Esta bien.	O.K.
🎧 INTRODUCING YOURSELF	
¿Cuál es tu nombre?	What is your name?
Mi nombre es Marta./Me llamo Marta.	My name is Martha.
Señor/Sr.	Mister/Mr.
Señora/Sra.	Missus/Mrs.
Señorita	Miss/Ms.
¡Mucho gusto en conocerte!	Nice to meet you!
¡Eres muy amable!	You're very kind!
¿De dónde eres?	Where are you from?

Spanish Popular Phrases	English Translation
Soy de México./Soy mexicano.	I'm from Mexico. I'm Mexican.
¿Cuánto tiempo llevas en U.S.?	How long have you been in the U.S.?
¿Dónde vives?	Where do you live?
Vivo en México.	I live in Mexico.
¿Le gusta a usted aquí?	Do you like it here?
¿A qué te dedicas?	What do you do for a living?
¿Cuántos años tienes?	How old are you?
¿Hablas inglés?	Do you speak English?
¿Hablas español?	Do you speak Spanish?
Solo un poquito.	Just a little.
🎧　　　TIME AND NUMBERS	
¿ A qué hora es mi cita?	What time is my appointment?
¿Qué hora es?	What time is it?
Son las once en punto.	It's 11 o'clock.
Mañana	Morning
Tarde	Afternoon

Spanish Popular Phrases	English Translation
Noche	Night
Mediodía	Noon
Uno, dos, tres	One, two, three
Cuatro, cinco, seis	Four, five, six
Siete, ocho, nueve, diez	Seven, eight, nine, ten

🎧 HOLIDAYS AND BEST WISHES

¡Feliz Día de las Madres!	Happy Mother's Day!
¡Feliz cumpleaños!	Happy birthday!
¡Feliz Año Nuevo!	Happy New Year!
¡Feliz Navidad!	Merry Christmas!
¡Felicidades!	Congratulations!
¡Buen provecho!	Enjoy it! (mostly used for meals)
¡Te deseo lo mejor!	I wish you the best!
¡Buen viaje!	Have a good trip!
¡Buena suerte!	Good luck!
Mis saludos/Dale mis saludos a (Mateo).	Say hi to Matthew for me.

Spanish Popular Phrases	English Translation
¡Salud!	Bless you (when sneezing)/Cheers (when making a toast)
¡Buenas noches!	Good night!

🎧 ASKING FOR HELP

Estoy perdido.	I'm lost.
¿Podría ayudarme, por favor?	Can you help me, please?
¿Puedo ayudarlo?	May I help you?
¡Necesito ayuda!	I need help!
¿Puede ayudarme con esta dirección?	Can you help with this address?
No puedo encontrar esta dirección.	I cannot find this address.
¿Cuánto vale?	How much is this?

🎧 ETIQUETTE AND CLARIFICATION

¡Disculpe!	Excuse me!
¡Lo siento!	Sorry.
¡No es problema!	No problem!
¡Puede repetirlo!	Can you say that again?

Spanish Popular Phrases	English Translation
¿Puede hablar más despacio, por favor?	Can you speak slowly, please?
¿Qué dijiste?	What did you say?
¿Estás seguro?	Are you sure?
¡No entiendo!	I don't understand!
¡No sé!	I don't know!
¡No estoy muy seguro!	I'm not very sure.
¡Firme aquí por favor!	Sign here, please!
¡Escríbalo, por favor!	Write it down, please!
¡No tengo idea!	I have no idea.
¿Qué es esto?	What is this?
Mi español es malo.	My Spanish is bad.
Me falta la práctica en español.	I need to practice my Spanish.
¡No se preocupes!	Don't worry!

🎧 IN THE DOCTOR'S OFFICE

Bienvenido/a.	Welcome.

Spanish Popular Phrases	English Translation
¿Cómo le puedo ayudar?	How may I help you?
¿Dígame que le pasa?	Tell me, what is going on?
¿Qué lo trae por aquí? (male patient) ¿Qué la trae por aquí? (female patient)	Why are you here today?
¿Es su primera cita?	Is this your first appointment?
Yo tengo dolor de espalda.	I have back pain.
¿Desde cuándo está enfermo?	How long have you been sick?
¿Está tomando algún medicamento?	Are you taking some medication?
¡Necesito un médico!	I need a doctor.
El doctor lo atenderá en unos minutos.	The doctor will be with you in a few minutes.
Hablo un poquito de español.	I speak a little Spanish.
Hábleme despacio por favor.	Speak slowly please.
Yo sé hablar español.	I know how to speak Spanish.
Yo hablo español.	I speak Spanish.
Más despacio	Slowly
No hablo español.	I don't speak Spanish.

Spanish Popular Phrases	English Translation
¿Dónde está el baño?	Where is the bathroom?
¿Dónde queda el consultorio médico?	Where is the doctor's office?
¡Vaya recto y vira a la derecha/izquierda!	Go straight then turn right/left!
Estoy buscando a la enfermera.	I'm looking for the nurse.
¡Un momento, por favor!	One moment, please!
¡No cuelgue, por favor!	Hold on, please! (phone)
Lo pondré en espera.	I'll put you on hold. (phone)
¡Perdóneme!	Excuse me! (to ask for something)
¡Perdone!/¡Disculpe!	Excuse me! (to pass by or if you make mistake)
¡Venga conmigo!	Come with me!
¡Sígame, por favor!	Follow me, please!
🎧 LANGUAGE PROBLEMS	
¿Habla inglés?	Do you speak English?
¿Me entiende?	Do you understand me?
No hablo muy bien el español.	I don't speak Spanish very well.

Spanish Popular Phrases	English Translation
Hable despacio, por favor.	Please speak slowly.
No entiendo.	I don't understand.
Por favor repítalo de nuevo.	Please say it one more time.
🎧 **QUESTIONS**	
¿Qué?	What?
¿Cómo?	How?
¿Qué pasa?	What is the matter?
¿Cuál?	Which?
¿Cuándo?	When?
Quién?	Who?
Por qué?	Why?
Cuánto?	How much is/are?
¿Puede usted ayudarme?	Can you help me?
¿Qué tan lejos?	How far?
¿Puede usted decirme?	Can you tell me?
¿Puede usted enseñarme?	Can you show me?

The following pages contain hundreds of phrases that will help you communicate with your Spanish-speaking patients. After reading through the ones that matter most to you, the goal will be to commit the most relevant phrases (for you) to memory. Any of the following options can work:

› Create index cards and/or posters (discussed in first section).

› Photocopy relevant pages and carry these around with you.

› Get a stack of sticky notes and put phrases on them. Place these notes where you will see them.

› Write simple songs using key phrases. If singing about something helps you remember it, get out that guitar and start strumming.

If you want to try something wackier than the ideas mentioned, that's fine; if you prefer to learn these phrases in a more traditional manner, knock yourself out. The point is, you'll want to do something more than just flip through this section one time. The actual method is not as important as doing something in addition to reviewing the phrases in this book once. After a bit of practice, you'll no longer need the index cards, the photocopied pages, or the lyrics of the song, but until you get to the point where you're comfortable recalling and saying the proper phrases, use whatever method works best for you.

HEY, I'VE SEEN THAT BEFORE!

As you go through the sections, you might see that we've occasionally repeated a phrase or two. We did this because our goal is to make learning these lists as easy as possible, so we've tried to keep related sentences together as much as possible. If we only wrote each phrase once, then you would often have to go flipping from one section to another simply because we didn't want to repeat the phrase: "Is there a chance you might be pregnant?" Sure, you might still do some page flipping every now and then, but if we could help make things simpler by just repeating a phrase or two, we did.

Also, keep in mind that *por favor* is "please" in Spanish. We placed it throughout the following pages many, many times, but truth be told, we could have added it even more. Use it whenever you can, *por favor*.

BASIC ANATOMY

This section on basic anatomy refers to common terms including body parts, organs, and organ systems that are often referred to by doctors, nurses, and other healthcare professionals.

We have strived to include the most common terms for both the healthcare professional and patient in an effort to decrease frustration for the patient and provider during a vulnerable time.

In some cases (depending on where the patient is from), more than one word can be utilized. We have included both words/terms where it applies.

English Term	Spanish Term	English Term	Spanish Term
🎧 COMMON TERMS		pupils	*las pupilas*
brain	*el cerebro*	eyebrows	*las cejas*
cranium	*el cráneo*	eyelashes	*las pestañas*
head	*la cabeza*	ears	*los oídos*
hair	*el cabello*	tympanic membrane	*la membrana timpánica*
forehead	*la frente*	nose	*la nariz*
chin	*la barbilla/el mentón*	nostrils	*la ventana de la nariz*
eyes	*los ojos*	cheek/cheeks	*la mejilla/los cachetes*

BASIC ANATOMY

English Term	Spanish Term	English Term	Spanish Term
jaw	*la mandíbula*	lungs	*los pulmones*
mouth	*la boca*	breasts	*los senos/las mamas*
gums	*las encías*	chest	*el pecho*
lips	*los labios*	nipples	*los pezones*
tongue	*la lengua*	areolas	*las areolas*
teeth	*los dientes*	stomach	*el estómago*
palate	*el paladar*	abdomen	*el abdomen*
molars	*las molares*	pubic region	*la zona púbica*
tonsils	*las amígdalas*	umbilical	*umbilical/el ombligo*
neck	*el cuello*	pancreas	*el páncreas*
esophagus	*el esófago*	gall bladder	*la vesícula biliar*
larynx	*la laringe*	liver	*el hígado*
heart	*el corazón*	spleen	*el bazo*
ribs	*las costillas*	appendix	*el apéndice*

English Term	Spanish Term	English Term	Spanish Term
kidneys	*los riñones*	lumbar region	*la región lumbar*
adrenal glands	*las glándulas suprarenales*	arms	*los brazos*
ureters	*los uréteros*	shoulders	*los hombros*
bladder	*la vejiga*	elbows	*los codos*
urethra	*la uretra*	hands	*las manos*
intestines large/small	*el intestino delgado/ grueso*	nails	*las uñas*
		fingers	*los dedos*
ascending/transverse/ descending colon	*el colon ascendente/ tranverso/descendente*	wrist	*la muñeca*
		biceps	*los bíceps*
rectum	*el recto*	triceps	*los tríceps*
bone marrow	*la médula ósea*	legs	*las piernas*
back	*la espalda*	thighs	*los muslos*
spine	*la columna vertebral*	knees	*las rodillas*
thoracic region	*la región torácica*	meniscus	*el menisco*

English Term	Spanish Term	English Term	Spanish Term
feet	*los pies*	blood	*la sangre*
toes	*los dedos del pie*	tissue	*el tejido*
quadriceps	*los cuádriceps*	organs	*los órganos*
hamstrings	*el ligamento de la corva*	skeletal system	*el sistema esquelético*
calves	*las pantorillas*	muscular system	*el sistema muscular*
Achilles tendon	*el tendon de Achilles*	circulatory system	*el sistema circulatorio*
skin	*la piel*	nervous system	*el sistema nervioso*
dermis	*el dermis*	respiratory system	*el sistema respiratorio*
bones	*los huesos*	digestive system	*el sistema digestivo*
nerves	*los nervios*	endocrine system	*el sistema endocrino*
muscles	*los músculos*	reproductive system	*el sistema reproductivo*
tendons	*los tendones*	lymphatic/immune system	*el sistema linfático/ inmunológico*
ligaments	*los ligamentos*		
cells	*las células*		

BASIC ANATOMY

English Term	Spanish Term
🎧 **SPECIFIC FEMALE ANATOMY**	
uterus	el útero/la matriz
ovaries	los ovarios
Fallopian tubes	la trompa de Falopio
cervix	el cuello del útero
vagina	la vagina
labia majora	los labios mayores
labia minora	los labios menores
🎧 **SPECIFIC MALE ANATOMY**	
penis	el pene
foreskin	el prepucio
circumcise	circuncidar
scrotum	el escroto
testicles	los testículos

English Term	Spanish Term
epididymis	el epidídimo
semen	el semen
🎧 **ANATOMY DURING PREGNANCY**	
pregnancy	el embarazo
placenta	la placenta
embryo	el embrión
lactation	la lactancia
umbilical cord	el cordón umbilical
gestation	la gestación
fetus	el feto
dilation	la dilatación
effacement	el borramiento
contraction	la contracción

SECTION: 3

BASIC ANATOMY

ADMISSION PROCESSES/GATHERING PATIENT INFORMATION

The section on admission processes and gathering patient information will help you in gathering health information from a patient or family member during a routine physical exam or a hospitalization. We have included common questions and phrases used when gathering patient information including personal information, history, and symptoms.

We have used the most common words for both healthcare professionals and patients alike. Although many of these terms are medical, most patients should be able to understand, as basic terms were used whenever possible.

English Phrase	Spanish Phrase
COMMON ADMISSION PHRASES	
Please fill out this admissions form.	*Por favor llene la forma de admisión.*
If you have any questions, please let me know.	*Si tiene algunas preguntas hágamelo saber.*
Please read and sign this consent form.	*Por favor lea y firme la forma de consentimiento.*
Your doctor will be _____.	*Su doctor estará _____.*
My name is _____ and I am your nurse.	*Mi nombre es _____ y yo soy su enfermera/o.*

English Phrase	Spanish Phrase
What is your preferred method of learning: reading, verbal, or demonstration?	¿Cuál es su método preferido de aprender: leyendo, verbal, o demostración?
How much do you weigh?	¿Cuánto pesa?
How tall are you?	¿Cuál es su estatura?
What is your race or ethnic background?	¿Cuál es su raza o étnica?
Please list any allergies to medications or foods.	Por favor incluya alergias a medicamentos o comidas.
Please list all of your medications, including non-prescription medications.	Por favor incluya todos sus medicamentos, incluyendo medicamentos sin receta.
Please list any childhood illnesses.	Por favor incluya enfermedades de la infancia.
Please list any accidents or injuries.	Por favor incluya todos sus accidentes y lesiones.
Please list any serious or chronic illnesses.	Por favor incluya enfermedades serias o crónicas.
Please list any hospitalizations.	Por favor incluya todas sus hospitalizaciones.
Please list any surgeries/operations.	Por favor incluya todas sus cirugías/operaciones.
For female patients: List last menstrual period, last gynecological exam and Pap smear. Was it normal or abnormal?	Pacientes femeninas: Incluya su última menstruación, último examen ginecológico, y último examen pap. ¿Fue normal o anormal?

English Phrase	Spanish Phrase
For female patients: List number of pregnancies, full term deliveries, preterm deliveries, number of incomplete pregnancies (abortions and miscarriages), and number of living children.	*Pacientes femeninas: Incluya número de embarazos, partos de término completo, partos de término incompleto, número de partos incompletos (abortos y abortos involuntarios), y número de hijos vivo.*
Please list if the births were vaginal or caesarean section deliveries.	*Por favor incluya si sus partos fueron vaginales o por operacíon cesárea.*
Please list all immunizations, including dates of last tuberculin test, tetanus immunization, and last flu shot.	*Por favor incluya sus vacunas, incluyendo su último examen tuberculínico, vacuna de tétano, y su última vacuna de la influenza.*
Please list your family history, including age and health or age and cause of death of blood relatives.	*Por favor incluya su historia médica familiar, incluyendo edad y estado de salud o edad y causa de muerte de sus parientes de sangre.*
What is your occupation? Are you exposed to any occupational hazards?	*¿Cual es su profesión/ocupación? ¿Es expuesto a algún peligro ocupacional?*
Please list highest level of education and financial status.	*Por favor incluya su nivel más alto de educación y estado económico.*
What is your marital status?	*¿Cuál es su estado civil?*

English Phrase	Spanish Phrase
Do you have children? If yes, how many and what are their ages?	¿Tiene hijos? ¿En caso afirmativo, cuántos y de qué edades?
What is your religious preference?	¿Cuál es su preferencia religiosa?
Do you exercise? If yes, what type?	¿Hace ejercicio? ¿Y qué tipo de ejercicio?
Please list sleeping habits, including naps, sleeping aids, and average hours of sleep.	Por favor incluya sus hábitos de dormir, incluyendo siestas, pastillas o otros remedios para dormir, y el promedio de horas que duerme.
Do you wear dentures?	¿Utiliza dentaduras?
Do you have any difficulty eating, chewing, or swallowing?	¿Tiene dificultad para comer, masticar, o tragar?
Do you have any nutritional needs?	¿Tiene una dieta especial o alguna otra necesidad nutricional?
Do you use tobacco? If so, how much and for how many years?	¿Utiliza tabaco? ¿Y cuánto y por cuántos años?
Do you drink alcohol? If so, how much?	¿Toma alcohol? ¿Y cuánto?
Do you use recreational drugs? If yes, what and how much?	¿Utiliza drogas recreativas? ¿Y cuánto y qué tipo?

English Phrase	Spanish Phrase
Do you feel safe at home?	*¿Se siente segura/o en su casa?*
Are you having pain? If yes, where is the pain located?	*¿Tiene dolor? ¿Y dónde tiene dolor?*
Can you describe the pain?	*¿Puede describir el dolor?*
When did the pain first start?	*¿Cuándo comenzó el dolor?*
On a one-to-ten pain scale, what would you rate your pain?	*¿En un escala del uno-a-diez, cómo clasifica su dolor?*
What makes the pain worse?	*¿Qué empeora el dolor?*
What makes the pain better?	*¿Qué mejora el dolor?*
Do you take anything for the pain? If so, what do you take?	*¿Toma algo para el dolor? ¿Y qué toma?*
Do you have any fever, chills, malaise, fatigue, or night sweats?	*¿Tiene fiebre, escalofríos, malestar, fatiga, o sudores?*
Have you had any recent weight gain or weight loss? If so, how many pounds?	*¿Ha perdida de peso o aumentado de peso? ¿Y cuántas libras?*
Do you have any headaches, dizziness, head injury, or loss of consciousness?	*¿Tiene dolores de cabeza, mareos, lesión a la cabeza, o pérdida de conocimiento?*

English Phrase	Spanish Phrase
Do you have any birthmarks, rashes, lesions, moles, or pigment changes?	¿Tiene marca de nacimiento, sarpullido, lesiones, lunares, o cambios de pigmento?
Do you have any nail or hair changes?	¿Tiene cambios en sus uñas o en su cabello?
Do you have vision changes, reading problems, eye discharge, double vision, or eye pain?	¿Tiene cambios en su visión, problemas para leer, desecho del ojo, visión doble, o dolor en el ojo?
Do you have any ear pain, drainage, tinnitus, vertigo, or hearing problems?	¿Tiene dolor de oído, desecho del oído, timbre en los oído, vértigo, o problemas para escuchar?
Do you use hearing aids?	¿Utiliza audífonos para escuchar?
Do you have any nasal congestion, drainage, nose bleeds, or sinus pain or pressure?	¿Tiene congestión nasal, desecho de la nariz, sangramiento de la nariz, o presión o dolor en los senos nasales?
Do you have any tooth problems, difficulty chewing or swallowing, oral lesions, sore throat, bleeding gums, hoarseness, tonsillectomy, or toothaches?	¿Tiene problemas en los dientes, problemas para masticar, tragar, lesiones bocales, dolor en la garganta, sangramiento de las encías, habla ronco, le removieron las amígdalas, o dolor en los dientes?
Do you have any neck stiffness or pain, or swollen glands?	¿Tiene alguna rigidez o dolor en el cuello, o inflamación de las glándulas?

English Phrase	Spanish Phrase
Have you performed a breast self-examination? Do you have any nipple discharge, breast lumps, or pain?	*¿Se hace un examen personal de los senos? ¿Tiene desecho de los pezones, bultos en los senos, o dolor en los senos?*
Do you have a cough (productive or non-productive), shortness of breath, wheezing, or asthma?	*¿Tiene tos (productiva o no productiva), dificultad para respirar, resollos, o asma?*
Do you have chest pain, palpitations, edema, weakness, cyanosis, difficulty breathing when lying flat, or heavy-feeling legs?	*¿Tiene dolor en el pecho, palpitaciones, edema o hinchazón de las piernas, decoloración azul en la piel, dificultad para respirar con estar acostado/a, o pesadez en las piernas?*
Do you have nausea, vomiting, abdominal pain, indigestion, diarrhea, constipation, blood in stool, or changes in stool?	*¿Tiene náuseas, vómito, dolor abdominal, indigestión, diarrea, estreñimiento, sangre en su excremento, o cambios en su excremento?*
Do you have frequency, urgency, pain, dysuria (burning with urination), hematuria (blood in urine), leakage, or difficulty urinating? Do you feel that you do not empty your bladder? Do you have kidney stones?	*¿Tiene la frecuencia, la urgencia, el dolor, la sangre, la orina, las fugas, o dificultad para orinar? ¿Se siente usted no vaciar su vejiga? ¿Tiene piedras en los riñones?*
For male patients: Do you have any penile, testicular, or scrotal pain, or penile discharge or lesions?	*¿Para pacientes masculinos: Tiene dolor del pene, de los testículos o del escroto, o desecho o lesiones del pene?*

English Phrase	Spanish Phrase
For female patients: When did menstruation start? Do you have any pelvic/cervical pain, vaginal discharge or odor, vaginal bleeding, or vaginal itching?	¿Para pacientes femeninas: A qué edad empezó su menstruación? Tiene dolor pélvico/cervical, desecho o mal olor vaginal, sangramiento vaginal, o picazón vaginal?
Are you sexually active? What is your sexual preference? Have you had any sexually transmitted diseases?	¿Es sexualmente activo/a? ¿Cuál es su preferencia sexual? ¿Ha tenido enfermedad de transmisión sexual?
Do you have any joint pain, swelling, redness, heat, stiffness, weakness, loss of coordination, or balance problems?	¿Tiene dolor, inflamación, enrojecimiento, calor, rigidez, debilidad, pérdida de coordinación, o su andar es desbalanceado?
Do you have any weakness, tics, seizures, numbness, or tingling?	¿Tiene debilidad, tics, ataques epilépticos, hormigueos, o adormecimiento de las extremidades?
Do you have excessive bruising or lymph gland swelling?	¿Tiene exceso de hematomas o hinchazón de las glándulas linfáticas?
Do you have excessive hunger, thirst, increased urination, hot or cold flashes, or abnormal hair distribution?	¿Tiene sed excesiva, hambre excesiva, orina excesivamente, bochornos o frío, o distribución anormal de cabello?

ADMISSIONS

MEDICAL FORMS (INSURANCE, PRIVACY, CONSENT)

Going to the doctor or being hospitalized can be a stressful event for the patient and family. Language barrier issues can add to the stress, especially when the patient and family cannot communicate with the healthcare professional and the medical forms that need to be filled out are in another language.

This section on medical forms will allow you to discuss a variety of common forms. These forms include surgical/procedure consents, Against Medical Advice (AMA) forms, and vaccination consents, to name a few. The most common phrases for filling out these forms have been included in this section.

English Term	Spanish Term
COMMON PHRASES	
Please fill out this form.	*Por favor llene esta forma.*
Do you need help filling out this form?	*¿Necesita ayuda para llenar la forma?*
Please include your full name.	*Por favor incluya su nombre completo.*
Please include your maiden name.	*Por favor incluya su apellido de soltera.*

English Term	Spanish Term
Please include any former name.	*Por favor incluya nombres pasados/antiguos.*
Please include your home address.	*Por favor incluya su dirección.*
Please include your home telephone number.	*Por favor incluya su número de teléfono.*
Please include an alternate number.	*Por favor incluya un número alternativo.*
Please include an emergency contact.	*Por favor incluya un contacto de emergencia.*
Please include your Social Security number.	*Por favor incluya su número de Seguro Social.*
Please include your e-mail address.	*Por favor incluya su correo electrónico.*
Are you a U.S. resident or citizen?	*¿Es ciudadano Americano o residente de los Estados Unidos?*
Please list your occupation.	*Por favor incluya su ocupación.*
Please list your employer, employer address, and telephone number.	*Por favor incluya su empleador, dirección de empleador, y número de teléfono.*
Please list your annual income.	*Por favor incluya sus ingresos anuales.*
Do you have medical insurance?	*¿Tiene seguro médico?*

English Term	Spanish Term
Please include your insurance information—identification number and group number.	*Por favor incluya la información de su seguro médico—incluyendo el numero de identificación y número del grupo.*
Do you have a health savings plan?	*¿Tiene un plan de ahorro de salud?*
Please list the amount of your deductible.	*Por favor incluya la cantidad de su deducible.*
How tall are you?	*¿Cuál es su estatura?*
How much do you weigh?	*¿Cuánto pesa?*
Do you smoke?	*¿Usted fuma?*
Are you a full-time college student?	*¿Es estudiante universitario de tiempo completo?*
We will need a blood sample.	*Necesitaremos un muestra de sangre.*
We will need a urine sample.	*Necesitaremos una muestra de orín.*
Do you have any pre-existing medical conditions?	*¿Tiene condiciones médicas preexistentes?*
Have you ever been diagnosed with cancer or an auto-immune disease?	*¿A sido diagnosticado con cáncer o una enfermedad autoinmune?*
Please read and sign this surgery consent.	*Por favor lea y firme esta consentimiento de cirugía.*

English Term	Spanish Term
What is the condition or diagnosis for which the test/surgery is recommended?	¿Cuál es la condición o diagnóstico por el cual se recomienda la prueba/la cirugía?
What does the test/surgery involve?	¿En qué consiste esta prueba/la cirugía?
What are the expected benefits of surgery?	¿Qué son los beneficios que puedo esperar de la prueba/la cirugía?
What are the possible risks of the test/surgery?	¿Qué son los posibles riesgos del examen/de la cirugía?
What are alternatives to the test/surgery?	¿Cuáles son las alternativas a la prueba/cirugía?
Please read and sign this procedure consent.	Por favor lea y firme el consentimiento para el procedimiento.
Please read and sign this blood transfusion consent.	Por favor lea y firme esta consentimiento de transfusión de sangre.
Have you had a previous adverse reaction to a blood transfusion?	¿Ha tenido una reacción adversa a una transfusión de sangre anteriormente?
Please fill out and sign the medical power of attorney.	Por favor llene y firme el poder notarial.
Please read and sign this Against Medical Advice document.	Por favor lea y firme este documento "Contra Advertencia Médica."

English Term	Spanish Term
Please read and sign this form: Do Not Resuscitate.	*Por favor lea y firme esta forma: No Resucitar.*
Please read and sign this vaccine consent: flu, tetanus, varicella (chicken pox), Gardisil (human papilloma virus), herpes zoster (shingles).	*Por favor lea y firme el consentimiento para la vacuna contra: la influenza, el tétano, la varicela, Gardisil (virus de papiloma humano), y herpes zoster (culebrilla).*
Please sign this release of records.	*Por favor lea y firme esta liberación de documentos médicos.*
Please read the Health Insurance Portability and Accountability Act (HIPAA) and let me know if you have questions.	*Por favor lea el acto de portabilidad y contabilidad de seguro médico y hágame saber si tiene preguntas.*
Please read the privacy acts and let me know if you have any questions.	*Por favor lea el acto de privacidad y hágame saber si tiene alguna pregunta.*
Please read and sign the pre-test counseling and consent for HIV testing.	*Por favor lea y firme esta forme de consejo antes de y consentimiento para el examen de la HIV.*
If you are under 18 years of age, please list name of parent or guardian.	*Si es menor de 18 años, por favor incluya el nombre de su padre/s o guardián.*
Patient Signature or Parent/Guardian Signature if under 18 years of age.	*Firma del paciente o Padre/Guardián si es menor de 18 años.*

English Term	Spanish Term
If you are not the patient, please state your relationship to the patient.	*Si no es usted el paciente, por favor incluya su relación al paciente.*
I have read and talked to my doctor about the test/surgery and understand the risks, benefits, and alternatives to the test/surgery.	*Yo he leído y hablado con mi doctor acerca de la prueba/cirugía y entiendo los posibles riesgos, beneficios, y alternativas a la prueba/cirugía.*
I know I may change my mind or refuse to have the test/surgery.	*Yo entiendo que puedo cambiar de opinión o rechazar la prueba/cirugía.*
If after reading the consent you do not agree with the above, please sign and date here.	*Si después de leer el consentimiento, no está de acuerdo con lo siguiente, por favor firme y incluya la fecha aquí.*
If after reading the consent you agree with the above and do not have any questions, please sign and date here.	*Si después de leer el consentimiento, está de acuerdo con lo siguiente y no tiene preguntas, por favor firme y incluya la fecha aquí.*
Please give us your driver's license to make a photocopy.	*Por favor déme su licencia de conducir para hacerle una fotocopia.*
I need a copy of all of your documents.	*Necesito una fotocopia de todos los documentos.*
Do you have a copy of your living will?	*¿Tiene una copia de su testamento?*

English Term	Spanish Term
Are you allergic to eggs, thimerosal (contact lens solution), have a history of Guillan-Barre, or have had a previous reaction to the flu shot?	*¿Es alérgico a los huevos, timerosal (solución de lentes de contacto), tiene una historia de Guillan-Barre, o ha tenido una reacción a la vacuna de la influenza?*
If you have a temperature/fever greater than 100.5, we will delay the vaccination.	*Si tiene una temperatura/fiebre más de 100.5, vamos a posponer la vacuna.*
Possible side effects include: tenderness at the site, fever, chills, headache, or muscle aches.	*Posibles efectos secundarios incluyen: dolor en el lugar de la inyección, fiebre, escalofríos, dolor de cabeza, o dolor en los músculos.*
Are you allergic to iodine?	*¿Es alérgico al yodo?*
Are you allergic to lidocaine?	*¿Es alérgico a la lidocaína?*
Who is your insurance carrier?	*¿Cuál es su cargador de seguro médico?*
Does your insurance cover dental and vision services?	*¿Sabe si su seguro médico cubre servicios dentales y de visión?*
What is your co-pay for your primary care provider?	*¿Cuál es su pago cuando visita a su doctor primario?*
What is your co-pay for specialist visits?	*¿Cuál es su pago cuando visita a un especialista?*
What is your co-pay for urgent care/emergency room visits?	*¿Cuál es su pago cuando va a un sala de urgencias/emergencias?*

MEDICAL TERMS

Medical terms are used in medical offices, hospitals, and other healthcare settings. This section will provide you with terms used in a variety of settings. These terms are as basic as naming an object, a procedure, or an exam.

English Phrase	Spanish Phrase
🎧 COMMON TERMS/PHRASES	
A syringe	*Una jeringa*
A needle	*Una aguja*
Do you have pain?	*¿Tiene dolor?*
I need to take your vital signs.	*Necesito tomarle los signos vitales.*
I need to take your blood pressure.	*Necesito tomarle la presión.*
I need to take your heart rate/pulse.	*Necesito tomarle su pulso.*
I need to take your temperature.	*Necesito tomarle la temperatura.*
I need your oxygen saturation.	*Necesito tomarle la saturación de oxígeno.*

English Phrase	Spanish Phrase
I need to get your weight.	*Necesito pesarlo/a.*
I need to get your height.	*Necesito su estatura.*

🎧 PROCEDURES

English Phrase	Spanish Phrase
We need to get laboratory studies.	*Necesitamos exámenes de laboratorio.*
We need a stool sample.	*Necesitamos una muestra de excremento.*
We need a urine sample.	*Necesitamos una muestra de orín.*
We need a blood sample.	*Necesitamos una muestra de sangre.*
We need to do a urine drug screen.	*Necesitamos un examen de orín para revisar drogas consumidas.*
You need testing for venereal diseases.	*Necesita un examen de enfermedades venéreas/transmitidas sexualmente.*
You need HIV testing.	*Necesita una prueba/un examen para la HIV que ocasiona el SIDA.*
We need to do a glucose check.	*Necesitamos revisarle la azúcar/glucosa.*
You will need an injection.	*Necesitará una inyección.*

English Phrase	Spanish Phrase
You will need an intravenous site (IV).	*Necesitará un suero intravenoso.*
You will need intravenous fluids.	*Necesitará líquidos/fluidos intravenosos.*
You will need a blood transfusion.	*Necesitará una transfusión de sangre.*
You will need a Foley catheter.	*Necesitará una sonda/catéter.*
You will need a breathing treatment.	*Necesitará un tratamiento respiratorio.*
You need oxygen.	*Necesita oxígeno.*
You need insulin.	*Necesita insulina.*
We need a throat culture.	*Necesitamos un cultivo de la garganta.*
We need a wound culture.	*Necesitamos un cultivo de su herida.*
You will need an enema.	*Necesitará una enema/lavativa.*
You will need a radiograph exam (x-ray).	*Necesitará un examen radiográfico (rayos-x).*
You will need an electrocardiogram (EKG).	*Necesitará un electrocardiograma.*
You will need an electroencephalogram (EEG).	*Necesitará un electroencefalograma.*
You will need computer tomography scan (CT-scan).	*Necesitará una tomografía computarizada.*

English Phrase	Spanish Phrase
You will need a magnetic resonance imaging exam (MRI).	*Necesitará una imagen de resonancia magnética.*
We need to do a stress test.	*Necesitamos hacerle un examen de tensión del corazón.*
You will need sutures.	*Necesitará suturas/puntadas.*
You will need staples.	*Necesitará grapas.*
We need to place a cast.	*Necesitamos ponerle un yeso.*
We need to cauterize.	*Necesitamos cauterizar.*
You will need a pelvic exam/pap smear.	*Necesitará un examen pélvico/Papanicolau.*
You will need a breast exam.	*Necesitará un examen de los senos.*
We need to perform an eye exam.	*Necesitamos hacerle un examen de los ojos.*
We need to perform a hearing test.	*Necesitamos hacerle un examen de los oídos.*
We need to perform a head-to-toe exam.	*Necesitamos hacerle un examen de pies a cabeza.*
We need to perform a neurological exam.	*Necesitamos hacerle un examen neurológico.*
We need to do a musculoskeletal exam.	*Necesitamos hacerle un examen muscular/óseo.*

English Phrase	Spanish Phrase
We need a biopsy.	*Necesitamos una biopsia.*
You will need surgery.	*Necesitará cirugía.*
This is a call light.	*Esto es un timbre.*
This is a stretcher/gurney.	*Esta es una camilla.*
This is an oxygen tank.	*Esto es un tanque de oxígeno.*
We need to listen to your lungs.	*Necesitamos escuchar sus pulmones.*
We need to listen to your abdomen.	*Necesitamos escuchar su abdomen/estómago.*
🎧	**POSSIBLE DIAGNOSES**
Your diagnosis is…….	*Su diagnóstico es…….*
You need a brace.	*Necesita un molde.*
You need crutches.	*Necesita unas muletas.*
You need a cane.	*Necesita un bastón.*
You need a walker.	*Necesita un andador.*
You are dehydrated.	*Está deshidratado.*

English Phrase	Spanish Phrase
You need antibiotics.	*Necesita antibióticos.*
You have a bacteria.	*Tiene una bacteria.*
You have a fungus.	*Tiene un hongo.*
You have a virus.	*Tiene un virus.*
You have pneumonia.	*Tiene pulmonía/neumonía.*
You have a cold.	*Tiene un resfriado.*
You have the flu.	*Tiene la influenza.*
You have a tumor.	*Tiene un tumor.*
You have a kidney stone.	*Tiene una piedra en el riñón.*
You have a dislocation.	*Tiene un dislocación.*
You have a fracture.	*Tiene una fractura.*
You have a laceration.	*Tiene una laceración/cortada.*
You have inflammation.	*Tiene inflamación.*
You have sepsis.	*Tiene sepsis, infección de la sangre.*

English Phrase	Spanish Phrase
You have a sprain.	*Tiene un esguince.*
You have a strain.	*Tiene una tensión.*
You have stenosis.	*Tiene estenosis.*
You have tachycardia.	*Tiene taquicardia.*
You have bradycardia.	*Tiene bradicardia.*
You have vasodilation.	*Tiene vaso dilatación.*
You have vasoconstriction.	*Tiene vaso constricción.*
You need a transplant.	*Necesita un transplante.*
You have withdrawal symptoms.	*Tiene síndrome de abstinencia.*
Your hemoglobin/hematocrit is low/high.	*Su hemoglobina/hematócrito está baja/alta.*
You are a carrier.	*Es un portador.*
You have immunity.	*Tiene inmunidad.*
Are you in labor?	*¿Tiene contracciones?*

SYMPTOMS AND FIRST MEETING

The previous lists covered some basic terms as well as the steps necessary to get a patient from the outer waiting room into a doctor's office or hospital room. Now that the patient is there, it's time to gather some general information as well as begin to take the patient's statement to find out why they decided they needed to see a doctor today.

As always, we've tried to place the phrases into groups that have some similarity.

English Phrase	Spanish Phrase
🎧 PHYSICAL EXAMINATION	
How tall are you?	¿Cuánto mide?
How much do you weigh?	¿Cuánto pesa?
How are you?	¿Cómo está usted?
Why are you here today?	¿Por qué está usted aquí hoy?
You seem anxious.	¿Usted parece ansioso.
You seem depressed.	¿Usted parece deprimido.

English Phrase	Spanish Phrase
Are you pregnant? Do you think there is any chance that you might be pregnant?	*¿Está embarazada? ¿Hay alguna posibilidad de que podría estar embarazada?*
Have you been drinking?	*¿Ha estado bebiendo?*
Have you taken any illegal drugs?	*¿Ha tomado alguna droga ilegal?*

🎧 PAIN

English Phrase	Spanish Phrase
Are you in pain?	*¿Tiene usted dolor?*
Where does it hurt?	*¿Dónde le duele?*
On a scale of 0 to 10, how bad is the pain?	*¿Usando una escala de cero a diez, qué fuerte es el dolor?*
Zero means no pain at all, 10 is the worst pain imaginable.	*Cero significa que no hay dolor; diez significa el peor dolor possible.*
Does it hurt all the time, or does the pain come and go?	*¿Le duele todo el tiempo, o el dolor se va y viene?*
When did the pain start?	*¿Cuándo empezó el dolor?*
What do you think caused the pain?	*¿Qué cree usted causó el dolor?*
Is there something that makes the pain worse?	*¿Hay algo que hace el dolor peor?*
Is there something that makes the pain better?	*¿Hay algo que hace el dolor mejor?*

SECTION 3

SYMPTOMS

English Phrase	Spanish Phrase
Does it hurt when I press here?	¿Le duele si le pulso aquí?
Can you describe the pain? Is it burning? Aching? Stabbing? Dull?	¿Puede describir el dolor? ¿Le arde? ¿Le duele? ¿Puñaladas? ¿Es dolor sordo?

🎧 MENTAL STATUS: BRIEF MENTAL STATUS EXAM

English Phrase	Spanish Phrase
I am going to ask you some questions now, okay?	¿Voy a hacerle algunas preguntas ahora, esta bien?
What is the date today?	¿Cuál es la fecha hoy?
What is the year?	¿En qué año estamos?
What is the season?	¿En qué estación del año estamos?
What is the month?	¿En qué mes estamos?
What is the day of the week?	¿En qué día de la semana estamos?
Where are we?	¿Dónde estamos?
What state are we in?	¿En qué estado estamos?
What town are we in?	¿En qué ciudad estamos?
What building/room are we in?	¿En que edificio/cuarto estamos?

English Phrase	Spanish Phrase
I am going to name three objects, and I want you to repeat them back to me. Apple, table, shoe.	*Voy a nombrar tres objetos, y quiero que usted los repita. Manzana, mesa, zapato.*
Can you repeat those objects to me?	*¿Puede repitirlos?*
I want you to remember them, because I am going to ask you to repeat them to me again later.	*Quiero que usted los recuerde, porque voy a pedirle a repetirlos otra vez dentro de unos minutos.*
I would like you to count backward by sevens, starting from 100.	*Me gustaría que cuente hacia atrás por sietes, a partir de cien.*
Can you spell "world" backward?	*¿Puede deletrear la palabra "mundo" hacia atrás?*
Do you remember those three objects we named a few minutes ago? Can you repeat them to me now?	*¿Recuerde usted los tres objetos que nombramos antes? ¿Puede repetirlos ahora?*
(Show a watch) What is this? (Answer: watch.)	*¿Cómo se llama? (reloj)*
(Show a pencil) What is this? (Answer: pencil.)	*¿Cómo se llama? (lapiz)*
I would like you to repeat the following: "No ifs, ands, or buts."	*Me gustaría que repita después de mí una frase: "Ni sí, ni no, ni pero."*
Take this paper in your right hand, fold it in half, and put it on the floor.	*Por favor, tome este papel en su mano derecha, doble el papel por la mitad, y ponga el papel en el piso.*

SYMPTOMS

English Phrase	Spanish Phrase
Read the following and do what it says: "Close your eyes."	*Lea las palabras de esta página, y haga luego lo que dice: "Cierre los ojos."*
Write a sentence for me on this piece of paper.	*Escriba una frase complete en esta hoja de papel.*
Please draw a clock.	*Por favor, dibuje un reloj.*
That is all, thank you.	*Eso es todo, gracias.*

 ## HEENT (HEAD, EYES, EARS, NOSE, THROAT)

Do you wear glasses or contacts?	*¿Usa usted lentes o contactos?*
Do you have difficulty seeing?	*¿Tiene problemas con su vista?*
Do you have difficulty reading?	*¿Tiene problemas leyendo?*
Please step over here and read the chart on the wall.	*Pase por aquí, por favor, y lea la carta en la pared.*
Can you read this line? This one?	*¿Puede leer esta línea? ¿Esta?*
I'm going to examine your eyes.	*Voy a examinar sus ojos.*
Do you have difficulty hearing?	*¿Tiene problemas para oír?*
Can you repeat the words I whisper to you?	*¿Puede repitir las palabras que susurro a usted?*

English Phrase	Spanish Phrase
Do your ears hurt?	¿Le duele sus oídos?
I'm going to look in your ears.	Voy a mirar en sus oídos.
Do you have nasal conjestion? Sinus pain or pressure?	¿Tiene congestión nasal? ¿Dolor o presión de seno?
Does your throat hurt?	¿Le duele la garganta?
Do you have difficulty eating or swallowing?	¿Tiene problemas para comer o tragar?
Open your mouth and say "AHH."	Abra la boca y diga "AHH."
Have you had a fever?	¿Ha tenido alguna fiebre?
Do you have headaches?	¿Tiene dolores de la cabeza?

🎧 CARDIOPULMONARY

English Phrase	Spanish Phrase
Do you have difficulty breathing?	¿Tiene dificultad respirando?
Do you have trouble breathing all of the time, or just sometimes?	¿Tiene dificultad respirando todo del tiempo, o solamente a veces?
Are you short of breath after exertion?	¿Le falta el aire después del esfuerzo?
What makes your breathing worse? What makes it better?	¿Qué hace que su respiración empeora? ¿Qué lo hace mejor?

SECTION 3

SYMPTOMS

English Phrase	Spanish Phrase
How long have you had problems breathing?	*¿Cuánto tiempo ha tenido usted problemas respirando?*
Do you have a history of problems with your lungs, like asthma or tuberculosis?	*¿Tiene una historia de problemas con sus pulmones, como asma o tuberculosis?*
Do you smoke?	*¿Usted fuma?*
Do you have a cough?	*¿Tiene tos?*
Are you bringing up phlegm when you cough?	*¿Existe flema al toser?*
Do you have a fever or a runny nose? A sore throat?	*¿Tiene fiebre o rinorrea? Le duele la garganta?*
Are you taking any medications?	*¿Está tomando medicamentos?*
Does it hurt to breathe?	*¿Le duele al respirar?*
I am going to listen to your lungs. Please breathe deeply and quietly while I am listening.	*Voy a escuchar a sus pulmones. Respire profundo y tranquilo mientras estoy escuchando.*
Will you please blow hard into this flow meter?	*¿Sopla duro, por favor, en este medidor de flujo?*
Do you have chest pain?	*¿Tiene dolor de pecho?*
Is the pain constant, or does it occur with certain activities?	*¿El dolor es constante, o ocurre solamente con algunas actividades?*

English Phrase	Spanish Phrase
Does the pain go away with rest?	¿El dolor desaparece con el descanso?
Do you tire easily?	¿Se cansa fácilmente?
Do you have a history of problems with your heart?	¿Tiene una historia de problemas del corazon?
Do you have a history of high blood pressure?	¿Tiene una historia de presión alta?
Have you ever fainted?	¿Alguna vez se ha desmayado?
Are you dizzy? Do you become dizzy when you stand up quickly?	¿Está mareado? ¿Alguna vez se siente mareado cuando se levanta rápidamente?
Do you have swelling in your legs and feet?	¿Tiene hinchazón en las piernas y los pies?
I'm going to listen to your heart now. Please breathe normally while I am listening.	Voy a escuchar a su corazon ahora. Por favor, respire normalmente mientras escucho.
We are going to do an EKG.	Vamos a hacer un electrocardiograma.
I am going to draw some blood for laboratory studies.	Voy a sacar sangre para estudios laboratorios.

🎧 ABDOMEN

Are you nauseous?	¿Tiene náusea?
Have you vomited?	¿Ha vomitado?

English Phrase	Spanish Phrase
Can you see food or coffee grounds in the vomit?	*¿Puede ver comida o posos de cafe en el vómito?*
Do you have diarrhea?	*¿Tiene diarrea?*
Are you able to keep water down?	*¿Puede mantener agua hacia abajo?*
Are you able to keep food down?	*¿Puede mantener alimentos hacia abajo?*
Are you constipated?	*¿Está estreñido?*
When was your last bowel movement?	*¿Cuándo fue su última evacuación intestinal?*
Are you passing gas?	*¿Está pasando gase?*
Do you have pain in your abdomen?	*¿Tiene dolor en la panza?*
Where does it hurt?	*¿Dónde le duele?*
Does it hurt when I press here?	*¿Le duele cuando le pulse aquí?*
How long have you had these symptoms?	*¿Cuánto tiempo hace que tiene estos síntomas?*
How is your appetite?	*¿Cómo es su apetito?*
Tell me about your diet.	*Dígame de su dieta.*

English Phrase	Spanish Phrase
🎧 **ELIMINATION**	
How often do you normally move your bowels?	*¿Con qué frecuencia se mueve sus intestinos normalmente?*
How are your stools now? Are they soft? Hard? Liquid? How are they normally?	*¿Como están sus heces ahora? ¿Están suaves? ¿Duros? ¿Como agua? ¿Como están normalmente?*
Do you see blood in the stool?	*¿Ve sangre en los heces?*
Does it hurt to pass stool?	*¿Le duele al pasar las heces?*
Are you having problems urinating?	*¿Tiene problemas orinando?*
Do you have a frequent, strong urge to urinate?	*¿Tiene las ganas de orinar frequente y fuerte?*
Does it hurt to urinate?	*¿Le duele a orinar?*
Do you feel like you have emptied your bladder when you urinate?	*¿Se siente que su vejiga está vacía después de haber orinado?*
What color is the urine?	*¿De qué color es la orina?*
Do you pass very large amounts of urine?	*¿Pasa grandes cantidades de orina?*
Are you unusually thirsty?	*¿Tiene más sed que normal?*

SECTION 3

SYMPTOMS

English Phrase	Spanish Phrase
SKIN	
How did you get this scar?	¿Como ocurrió esta cicatriz?
Do you have a rash?	¿Tiene usted una erupción?
Does it itch? Is it painful?	¿Le pican? ¿Es dolorosa?
How long have you had this rash?	¿Desde hace cuándo ha tenido esta erupción?
Did you have any symptoms of illness before the rash appeared?	¿Tuvo síntomas de enfermedad antes de la erupción?
Have you recently taken any antibiotics?	¿Ha tomado recientemente cualquier antibióticos?
Have you been exposed to any harsh chemicals?	¿Ha estado expuesto a productos químicos fuertes?
Have you been working outside?	¿Ha estado trabajando afuera?

ILLNESSES

The phrases in this section cover some of the common statements you might make to a patient diagnosed with that illness. Some statements help explain the condition; others discuss steps the patient can take if conditions worsen. In general, the goal is to provide patients with the information necessary to help them get better.

English Phrase	Spanish Phrase
UPPER RESPIRATORY INFECTIONS	
The common cold is a viral infection of the nose, throat, and upper airways.	*El resfrío es un infección viral de la nariz, la garganta, y las vías respiratorias superiores.*
Symptoms usually start with irritation of the nose and throat and progress to nasal congestion, sneezing, sore throat, and coughing. Fever is rare.	*Los síntomas normalmente empiezan con inflamada de la nariz y la garganta, y avanzan, a la congestión nasal, los estornudos, el dolor en la garganta, y tos. La fiebre es rara.*
Symptoms usually last 5 to 10 days and resolve without treatment. A mild cough may persist for two weeks.	*Los síntomas usualmente duran cinco a diez días y se desparecen sin tratamiento. Una leve tos puede persistir durante dos semanas.*

English Phrase	Spanish Phrase
Influenza, or the flu, is a viral illness with symptoms similar to the common cold. Influenza symptoms are usually worse and may be accompanied by fever and aching muscles and joints.	*La influenza, o la gripe, es una enfermedad viral con síntomas similares al resfrío. Los síntomas de la influenza usualmente son peor, y están acompañados de fiebre y dolores en los músculos y las articulaciones.*
In a healthy individual, influenza usually resolves without complications or medications.	*En una persona saludable, la influenza generalmente se resuelve sin complicaciones o medicamentos.*
Both colds and the flu are highly contagious, and are spread by contact with the phlegm and saliva of infected individuals.	*El resfrío y la influenza son muy contagiosos, y se propagan por el contacto con la flema y la saliva de las personas infectadas.*
Handwashing is the most important means of preventing the spread of these illnesses.	*Lavando las manos es lo más importante de los métodos de prevención de la propagación de estas enfermedades.*
You should see your doctor if fever greater than 102 degrees persists for more than three days, if you have difficulty breathing, or if you get better for a while and then get worse.	*Debe consultar a su médico si usted tiene fiebre superior a ciento y dos grados por más de tres días, si tiene dificultad respirando, o si se mejora y luego empeora.*

English Phrase	Spanish Phrase
Elderly people, people with HIV or other immune deficiencies, and young children are at risk for complications from influenza, and should see a doctor if they have symptoms.	*Las personas de edad avanzada, las personas con HIV y otras inmunodeficiencias, y los niños pequeños están en riesgo de complicaciones de la influenza, y deben consultar con su médico si tienen síntomas.*
Those at risk for complications from influenza should receive a yearly flu vaccine in the fall.	*Ellos en riesgo de complicaciones de la influenza deben recibir una vacuna cada año en el otoño.*

LOWER RESPIRATORY TRACT INFECTIONS

Tuberculosis is a bacterial infection that occurs most commonly in the lungs. It is highly contagious.	*La tuberculosis es una infección bacterial que ocurre especialmente en los pulmones. Es muy contagioso.*
Ninety percent of people who are infected with tuberculosis will not develop the active disease.	*El noventa por ciento de las personas infectadas con tuberculosis no se desarrolla una enfermedad activa.*
Tuberculosis can be treated, but it requires antibiotics taken for 6 to 12 months.	*La tuberculosis se puede tratar, pero hay que tomar antibióticos durante seis a doce meses.*
People who fail to complete this very long treatment risk developing a form of tuberculosis that is resistant to antibiotics.	*Las personas que no completan este tratamiento muy largo están en riesgo de desarrollando una forma de tuberculosis que es resistente a los antibióticos.*

SECTION 3

ILLNESSES

English Phrase	Spanish Phrase
If you have been in close contact with someone with tuberculosis, or if you have symptoms of tuberculosis, you should see your doctor.	*Si usted ha estado en contacto con alguien con tuberculosis, o si tiene los síntomas de tuberculosis, debe consultar con su médico.*
Symptoms of tuberculosis include a cough, sometimes with bloody sputum, chest pain, breathlessness, and night sweats.	*Los síntomas de tuberculosis incluyen tos, a veces con flema sangrado, dolor en el pecho, dificultad respirar, y sudor durante la noche.*
Pneumonia results from infection of the lower lungs. While fighting the infection, the body creates pus that collects in the airways and makes breathing difficult.	*La neumonía es una infección del los pulmones inferiores. Mientras lucha contra la infección, el cuerpo crea pus que se acumula en las vías respiratorias y hace difícil la respiración.*
Pneumonia can be caused by a virus or a bacteria. Bacterial infections require treatment with antibiotics.	*La neumonía puede ser causada de un viro o bacterias. Infecciones bacteriales necesitan tratamiento con los antibióticos.*
Symptoms of pneumonia include blue lips and fingernails, difficulty breathing, pain on breathing, chest discomfort or pain, chills, fever, and cough.	*Los síntomas de neumonía incluyen un color azul de los labios y los dedos, dificultad respirando, dolor con las respiraciones, dolor en el pecho, resfriados, fiebre, y tos.*
You should see your doctor if you think you have pneumonia.	*Debe consultar a su doctor si crea que tiene la neumonía.*

English Phrase	Spanish Phrase

NAUSEA/VOMITING/DIARRHEA

Nausea, vomiting, and diarrhea can be symptoms of many kinds of illnesses.	*La náusea, los vómitos, y la diarrea pueden ser síntomas de muchas clases de enfermedades.*
Most often, these symptoms resolve in a few days. Medicines are not needed.	*La mayoría de las veces, estos síntomas desaparecen en pocos días. No se necesita las medicinas.*
The most important treatment for these symptoms is to drink plenty of fluids. Vomiting and diarrhea can lead to dehydration, especially in the elderly and young children.	*El más importante tratamiento por estos síntomas es beber abundante líquidos. Los vómitos y la diarrea pueden causar la deshidratación, especialmente en las personas de edad avanzada y los niños pequeños.*
Rest the stomach and intestines for several hours, then begin drinking clear fluids.	*Descanse el estómago por varias horas, y entonces empieze a tomar líquidos claros.*
If you cannot keep liquids down, or if you have frequent, severe diarrhea, you need to see a doctor.	*Si no puede retener los líquidos o si tiene diarrea frecuente y severa, debe consultar con su médico.*

FEVER

Fever is one of the body's methods of fighting illness. It can be a symptom of many conditions, most of them mild.	*La fiebre es uno de los métodos que tiene el cuerpo para luchar contra la enfermedad. Puede ser un síntoma de muchas condiciones, la mayoría suaves.*

SECTION 3

ILLNESSES

English Phrase	Spanish Phrase
Fever often rises every four to six hours, then returns to normal.	*A menudo la fiebre aumenta cada cuatro o seis horas, y luego vuelve a la normalidad.*
Fever can make you feel very ill, and can cause vomiting and dehydration.	*La fiebre puede hacerle sentir muy enfermo, y puede causar vómitos y deshidratación.*
Treat fever with Tylenol and tepid baths. Drink plenty of water and other fluids. Rest.	*Trate la fiebre con Tylenol y baños tibios. Tome abundante agua y otros líquidos. Descanse.*
High fever in children can sometimes cause seizures. This should be reported to your doctor.	*La fiebre alta a veces puede causar los ataques en los niños. Esto debe ser comunicado a su médico.*
Never give aspirin to children to treat fever. Give Tylenol or Motrin.	*Nunca dé aspirina a los niños con fiebre. Deles Tylenol o Motrin.*

URINARY TRACT INFECTIONS

Urinary tract infections are caused by bacteria entering the urethra and bladder, most often from the rectum.	*Las infecciones urinarias son causadas por bacterias que se introduzcan en la uretra y la vejiga, la mayoría de las casos del recto.*
Urinary tract infections are most common in women.	*Las infecciones urinarias son más comunes en las mujeres.*

English Phrase	Spanish Phrase
Symptoms of a urinary tract infection include a strong, frequent urge to urinate, a burning sensation while urinating, or blood in the urine.	*Los síntomas de una infección urinaria incluyen las ganas fuertes y frequentes a orinar, una quemazón mientras orinar, o sangre en la orina.*
If you have symptoms of a urinary tract infection, you should see your doctor for treatment.	*Si usted tiene los síntomas de una infección urinaria, debe consultar con su médico para tratamiento.*
Urinary tract infections can be prevented by good hygiene. Wipe from front to back. Wear cotton underwear. Avoid douching.	*Las infecciones urinarias pueden ser prevenidas con una buena higiene. Se limpie de adelante hacia atrás. Use ropa interior de algodón. No use ducha vaginal.*

SKIN CONDITIONS

English Phrase	Spanish Phrase
Lice are tiny insects that live on the hairy parts of the human body, most often the head and the groin.	*Los piojos son insectos pequeños que viven en el pelo del cuerpo humano, la mayoría de las veces en la cabeza o en la ingle.*
Lice can be seen moving in the hair, and their eggs look like specks of salt stuck to the root of the hair.	*Los piojos se pueden ver moviendo en el pelo, y sus huevos parecen granos de sal, pegados a las raíces del pelo.*
They cause itching, and the skin may be reddened from scratching.	*Ellos causan comezón, y la piel puede ser de color rojo debido a arañazos.*

English Phrase	Spanish Phrase
Lice are very contagious. Children frequently contract them at school.	*Los piojos son muy contagiosos. Los niños a menudo los obtienen en la escuela.*
Treatment of lice includes washing with a medicated shampoo that you can buy at the pharmacy, followed by careful combing of the hair to remove lice eggs.	*El tratamiento de piojos incluye lavando con un champú medicado, que se puede comprar en la farmacia, seguido de un peinado cuidadoso del cabello para eliminar los huevos.*
Monitor all household members for lice, and treat them too if insects or eggs are noted.	*Supervise todos los miembros del hogar para los piojos; trate de ellos también si se observan los insectos o los huevos.*
Wash all household bed linens, towels, combs, brushes, hats, and clothing with hot water and soap.	*Lave todas las ropas de camas, toallas, peines, cepillos, sombreros, y ropas que pueden estar contaminados con agua caliente y jabón.*
Treatments may need to be repeated. Reinfection is common.	*Puede ser necesario a repetir los tratamientos. Reinfección es común.*
Scabies is an infestation of the skin by tiny insects. They burrow under the skin and cause itching, often all over the body.	*La sarna es una infestación de la piel por insectos pequeños. La sarna madriguera debajo de la piel y causa comezón, a menudo en todo el cuerpo.*

English Phrase	Spanish Phrase
Treatment is the application of a medicated cream, which is rubbed all over the body and left on for several hours.	*El tratamiento es la aplicación de una crema medicada, que se frota en todo el cuerpo y dejado puesto por horas varias.*
Scabies is very contagious. All family members must be treated. All bed linens, towels, and clothing must be washed with hot water and soap.	*La sarna es muy contagiosa. Todos en la familia tienen que recibir tratamiento. Todas las ropas de camas, toallas, y ropa deben ser lavado con agua caliente y jabón.*
Poison ivy is a rash that is caused by contact with a common plant.	*El zumaque es una erupción cutánea que se produce por contacto con una planta.*
The rash is characterized by reddened skin and little blisters filled with watery pus. It is itchy and painful.	*La erupción se caracteriza en la piel rojiza y ampollas llenas de un pus aguado. Es muy picosa y dolorosa.*
The rash can spread if you scratch it and then touch other parts of your body with your infected hands. Try not to scratch.	*La erupción puede extenderse si se la rasca y toca otras partes del cuerpo con sus manos infectadas. Trate de no rascarse.*
Wash the rash thoroughly with soap and hot water. Then wash your hands. Wash any clothing you think might have come in contact with the plant.	*Lave la erupción con jabón y agua caliente. Después, lave sus manos. Lave cualquier ropa que piensa que ha contactada la planta.*
Treat the rash with cortisone cream, which you can buy at the pharmacy.	*Trate la erupción con una crema de cortisona, que se puede comprar en la farmacia.*

English Phrase	Spanish Phrase
Sometimes the rash may be so severe that cortisone pills are needed. See your doctor if this occurs.	*A veces, la erupción puede ser tan severa que pastillas de cortisona son necesarias. Consulte con su médico si esto ocurre.*
Poison ivy can also spread into the eyes, nose, throat, and airways. This condition should be treated by a doctor.	*El zumaque puede entrar en los ojos, la nariz, la garganta y las vías respiratorias. Esta condición debe ser tratado por un médico.*

ANEMIA

English Phrase	Spanish Phrase
The most common type of anemia is iron deficiency.	*El más común tipo de la anemia es una deficiencia del hierro.*
Iron deficiency can occur during the times of life when the body needs extra iron, such as during pregnancy or the rapid growth of childhood.	*La deficiencia del hierro puede ocurrir durante los momentos de la vida cuando el cuerpo necesita el hierro extra, como durante el embarazo o el crecimiento rápido de la infancia.*
Iron deficiency can also be caused by poor nutrition, by a lack of iron in the diet.	*La deficiencia del hierro puede ser causada por la mala nutrición, la falta del hierro en la dieta.*
Symptoms of anemia include feeling tired and weak, a pale appearance, poor concentration, and susceptibility to illness.	*Los síntomas de la anemia incluyen sintiendo cansado y débil, un aspecto pálido, falta de concentración, y susceptibilidad a la enfermedad.*

English Phrase	Spanish Phrase
Your doctor may prescribe iron, or you can buy iron tablets from the pharmacy.	*Su médico puede recetar el hierro, o se puede comprar pastillas del hierro de la farmacia.*
You should eat foods rich in iron, including red meats, shellfish, beans, tomatoes, and spinach.	*Debe comer alimentos ricos en el hierro, incluyendo las carnes rojas, los mariscos, los frijoles, los tomates y las espinacas.*

ASTHMA

English Phrase	Spanish Phrase
Asthma is a disease of the airway of the lungs. During an attack, the airways constrict and produce mucus, making the passage of air in and out of the lungs difficult.	*El asma es una enfermedad de las vías respiratorias en los pulmones. Durante un ataque, las vías respiratorias contraen y producen una mucosidad, haciendo difícil la entrada y salida del aire en los pulmones.*
Symptoms of asthma include wheezing, shortness of breath, pressure in the chest, and a cough, especially at night or early in the morning.	*Los síntomas del asma incluyen la sibilancia, falta del aire, presión en el pecho, y tos, especialmente en la noche o temprano en la mañana.*
Asthma is a chronic condition, but attacks usually occur only occasionally.	*La condición del asma es crónica, pero los ataques ocurren solamente periódicamente.*
An asthma attack is often triggered by exposure to allergens such as pollen or tobacco smoke.	*Un ataque del asma puede ser causado cuando se expone a agentes environmentales, como polen o humo del tabaco.*

English Phrase	Spanish Phrase
An asthma attack may be triggered by exercise or stress, or by illness like cold or flu.	*Un ataque de la asma puede estar causado de ejercicio físico, presión, o de enfermedades como la gripe o la influenza.*
You can control your asthma symptoms by taking anti-inflammatory medications prescribed by your doctor on a regular basis.	*Se puede controlar los síntomas del asma tomando medicamentos contra inflamación recetados por su doctor regularmente.*
You can relieve an asthma attack by using an inhaled medication prescribed by your doctor when symptoms occur.	*Se puede aliviar un ataque del asma utilizando un medicamento inhalado, recetado por su doctor, cuando los síntomas ocurren.*
If medications are not working and you continue to have difficulty breathing, you must call your doctor or go to the emergency room.	*Si los medicamentos no funcionen, si continúa a tener dificultad respirando, debe llamar a su doctor o ir a la sala de emergencias.*

ARTHRITIS

Arthritis is inflammation of the joints.	*La artritis es la inflamación de las articulaciones.*
Arthritis can be caused by a number of conditions, including genetics, disease, and injury. Often the cause is unknown.	*La artritis puede ser causada por condiciones varias, incluyendo las genéticas, las enfermedades, y lesiones. Muchas veces no sabemos la causa.*

English Phrase	Spanish Phrase
The most common type of arthritis is osteoarthritis—deterioration of the bones and loss of fluid in the joints.	*El más común tipo de la artritis es osteoartritis—la deterioración de los huesos y la pérdida del líquido en las articulaciones.*
Symptoms of arthritis are pain and swelling in the joints, especially the hands, hips, and knees.	*Los síntomas de la artritis son dolor y hinchazón en las articulaciones, especialmente en las manos, la cadera, y las rodillas.*
Arthritis is a chronic condition, and there is no cure.	*La artritis es una condición crónica, y no hay cura.*
Take care of your arthritis by using pain medications like Tylenol when necessary. If you are taking a lot of Tylenol, you should talk to your doctor about other types of medications.	*Cuídese de su artritis tomando medicinas para el dolor, como Tylenol, cuando es necesario. Si usted está tomando mucho del Tylenol, debe hablar con su médico acerca de otros tipos de medicamentos.*
Physical activity is the most important therapy for arthritis. You should try to get thirty minutes of moderate exercise three times a week.	*La actividad física es la terapia más importante por la artritis. Debe tratar de obtener al menos treinta minutos de ejercicio tres veces a la semana.*
Many people find that water exercise is a gentle way to improve the function of the joints.	*Muchas personas encuentran que el ejercicio en la agua es una manera suave para mejorar la función de las articulaciones.*

English Phrase	Spanish Phrase
CANCER	
Cancer is the name for more than 100 illnesses characterized by uncontrolled growth of cells in the body.	*El cáncer es el nombre de más de cien enfermedades caracterizadas por el crecimiento incontrolado de las células en el cuerpo.*
In cancer, cells stop functioning normally. They enlarge and multiply at a rapid rate, often forming a mass of abnormal cells called a tumor.	*En el cáncer, las células no funcionan normalmente. Amplían y se multiplican a un ritmo rápido, a menudo formando una masa de las células anormales llamada un tumor.*
Uncontrolled growth can occur in almost any tissue of the body: the lungs, the brain, the skin, and the blood. That is why there are so many different kinds of cancer.	*El crecimiento incontrolado puede ocurrir en casi cualquier tejido del cuerpo: los pulmones, el cerebro, la piel, y la sangre. Por eso hay muchos tipos diferentes de cáncer.*
There are many common screening procedures for cancer, such as the mammogram and the Pap smear.	*Hay muchas pruebas de cribado comunes para el cáncer, como la mamografía y el examen Pap.*
Treatment for cancer is most effective if it is discovered early. That is why screening procedures are so important.	*El tratamiento para el cáncer es más efectivo si es descubierto temprano. Por eso las pruebas de cribado están tan importantes.*

English Phrase	Spanish Phrase
If left untreated, cancer can cause serious illness and death.	*Si se deja sin tratamiento, el cáncer puede causar enfermedades graves o la muerte.*
Different types of cancer respond best to different types of treatments. Treatments for cancer include radiation, chemotherapy, and surgery.	*Diferentes tipos de cáncer responden mejor a diferentes tratamientos. Los tratamientos para el cáncer incluyen la radioterapia, la quimioterapia, y la cirugía.*
Symptoms of cancer can include:	*Los síntomas de cáncer pueden incluir:*
weight loss	*pérdida de peso*
fatigue	*fatiga*
changes in the skin, moles, or freckles	*cambios en la piel, lunares, o pecas*
a lump in the breast or testicles, or another part of the body	*un bulto en la mama o los testículos, o en otra parte del cuerpo*
unusual bleeding in the sputum, stool or from the vagina	*la sangre inusual en el esputo, los heces, o de la vagina*
pain	*dolor*
difficulty swallowing	*dificultad para tragar*
hoarseness or cough that won't go away	*ronguera o tos que no desaparece*

English Phrase	Spanish Phrase
These symptoms do not mean you have cancer, but you should report them to your doctor.	*Estos síntomas no indican que tiene el cáncer, pero debe informarlos a su médico.*

CHRONIC OBSTRUCTIVE PULMONARY DISEASES (COPD)

English Phrase	Spanish Phrase
Emphysema is a chronic condition characterized by damage to the lungs. The most common cause is smoking.	*La enfisema es una enfermedad crónica caracterizada por daño a los pulmones. La causa más común es el fumar.*
Prolonged exposure to smoke or other substances like coal dust can cause changes to the lungs that obstruct airflow and make it difficult to exhale.	*La exposición prolongada al humo u otras sustancias como el polvo de carbón causa cambios en los pulmones que resultan en obstrucción y hacen difícil a exhalar.*
Symptoms of emphysema include shortness of breath, a chronic cough, a blue color around the lips and fingernails, and the need to get in a supported position to breathe easily.	*Los síntomas de la enfisema incluyen dificultad respirando, tos crónica, color azul cerca de los labios y los dedos, y la necesidad de sentarse en una posición suportada para respirar fácilmente.*
The most important treatment for emphysema is to stop smoking.	*El tratamiento más importante para la enfisema es dejar de fumar.*
Other treatments include inhaled steroids, antibiotics, and oxygen.	*Otros tratamientos incluyen los esteroides inhalados, antibióticos, y el oxígeno.*

English Phrase	Spanish Phrase
DIABETES	
Diabetes is a nutritional disorder.	*La diabetes es un trastorno nutricional.*
When we eat, the body converts much of our food into glucose, or sugar, that is burned for energy.	*Cuando comemos, el cuerpo cambia mucho de los alimentos a glucosa, o el azúcar, que se quema para producir energía.*
Glucose enters the bloodstream from the intestines and is carried to the cells to be burned.	*La glucosa penetra en el torrente sanguíneo desde el intestino y se lleva a las células para ser quemado.*
The hormone insulin works to move the sugar from the bloodstream into the cells.	*La hormona insulina funciona a mover el azúcar desde el torrente sanguíneo a las células.*
In one type of diabetes, the body does not make insulin. Insulin must be taken by injection in order to survive. This type of diabetes is most common among children.	*En un tipo de la diabetes, el cuerpo no se produce la insulina. La insulina tiene que ser tomado por inyección para sobrevivir. Esto tipo de la diabetes es más común en los niños.*
In the second type of diabetes, the cells are resistant to the insulin, and the insulin does a poor job of moving the sugar from the blood into the cells. This type is more common in adults.	*En el segundo tipo de la diabetes, las células son resistentes a la insulina, y la insulina no funciona bien a mover el azúcar desde la sangre hasta las células. Este tipo es más común en los adultos.*

English Phrase	Spanish Phrase
In both types of insulin, the body is poorly nourished, and high levels of sugar circulate in the bloodstream, unable to enter the cells.	*En los dos tipos de la diabetes, el cuerpo está mal nutrido, y niveles altos de azúcar circule en la sangre, pero no pueden entrar en las células.*
Glucose is a big molecule, and it tears up the tiniest, most delicate blood vessels as it moves through them, causing permanent damage.	*La glucosa es una molécula grande, y causa daño a los vasos sanguíneos más pequeños y delicados a medida que se mueve a través de ellos.*
It is damage to the blood vessels that causes complications of diabetes.	*Es el daño a los vasos sanguíneos que causa las complicaciones de diabetes.*
Damage to the vessels of the eyes causes blindness.	*El daño a los vasos de los ojos causa la ceguera.*
Damage to the vessels of the hands, feet, and legs results in swelling, loss of sensation, and poor healing of wounds.	*El daño a los vasos de las manos, los pies, y las rodillas resulta en hinchazón, pérdida de sensación, y mala cicatrización de las heridas.*
Damage to the vessels of the kidneys causes kidney disease.	*El daño a los vasos de los riñones causa enfermedad de los riñones.*
Diabetes can sometimes be controlled with changes in diet, combined with weight loss and exercise.	*A veces, la diabetes puede ser controlada con cambios en la dieta, junto a la pérdida de peso y el ejercicio.*

English Phrase	Spanish Phrase
If diet and exercise are not enough, medication or insulin is necessary.	*Si la dieta y el ejercicio no son suficientes, los medicamentos o la insulina son necesarios.*
It is very important to follow all instructions for diet, exercise, and medication, to check your blood sugar regularly, and to see your doctor often.	*Es muy importante seguir todas las instrucciones de dieta, ejercicio, y medicamentos, vigilar el nivel de azúcar en su sangre con regularidad, y ver a su médico con frecuencia.*
The goal of treatment is to keep blood sugar levels normal, to improve nutrition, and to prevent complications of diabetes.	*El objetivo del tratamiento es mantener los niveles normales de azúcar en la sangre, para mejorar la nutrición, y para prevenir las complicaciones de la diabetes.*

EPILEPSY

English Phrase	Spanish Phrase
Epilepsy is a condition of the nervous system that causes intermittent disturbances to the normal function of the brain, resulting in seizures.	*La epilepsia es una enfermedad del sistema nervioso que periódicamente causa perturbaciones de la función normal del cerebro, dando lugar a los ataques epilépticos.*
A person who has had two or more seizures is said to have epilepsy.	*Una persona que ha tenido dos o más ataques tiene la epilepsia.*

English Phrase	Spanish Phrase
Most people think of seizures as convulsions, and these are very common, but there are other types of seizures, like absence seizures, when the mind just goes blank and the person stares off into space.	*La mayoría de la gente considera los ataques como convulsiones, y éstas son muy comunes, pero hay otros tipos de ataques, como ataques de ausencia, cuando la mente se pone en blanco y la persona sólo mira hacia el espacio.*
Most seizures last a minute or two. The person may lose consciousness. Often after a seizure, the person will be confused and may say things that make no sense.	*La mayoría de los ataques duran uno o dos minutos. La persona puede perder el conocimiento. A menudo, después de un ataque, la persona está confundida y dice cosas absurdas.*
If you care for someone who has seizures, the most important thing is to keep the person safe while the seizure is occurring. Lower the person to the ground, and move objects out of their way.	*Si usted da cuidas a alguien con epilepsia, la cosa más importante es para mantener la persona segura cuando la convulsión ocurre. Mueve la persona al piso, y mueve objetos fuera del peligro.*
A seizure lasting more than five minutes is an emergency. Call 911.	*Una convulsión que dura más de cinco minutos es una urgencia. Llame a 911.*
Epilepsy can often be controlled with medications. It is important to take the medications regularly and to stay in contact with your doctor.	*Muchas veces, la epilepsia puede ser controlada con medicamentos. Es importante tomar los medicamentos con regularidad y mantener contacto con su médico.*

English Phrase	Spanish Phrase
Getting plenty of sleep, good nutrition, and decreasing stress can also reduce the occurrence of seizures.	*Mucho sueño, la nutrición buena, y la reducción del estrés también pueden reducir la frecuencia de los ataques.*
Seizures can still occur, even if you are taking good care of yourself and taking your medications properly.	*Los ataques pueden ocurrir todavía, incluso si usted está tomando buen cuidado de si mismo y tomando sus medicamentos con regularidad.*
People with epilepsy may be restricted from driving.	*Las personas con epilepsia pueden restringirse de conducir.*

HEART DISEASE AND STROKE

There are many types of heart disease, including congenital conditions, but usually when people say heart disease they are talking about conditions that can lead to a heart attack.	*Hay muchos tipos de las enfermedades del corazón, pero generalmente cuando se dicen enfermedad del corazón, significan las condiciones que pueden conducir a un ataque al corazón.*
The most common condition that can lead to a heart attack is atherosclerosis.	*La condición más común que puede conducir a un ataque al corazón es la aterosclerosis.*
In atherosclerosis, the arteries become blocked by deposits of fat and plaque, narrowing the diameter of the bloodstream and reducing blood flow.	*En la aterosclerosis, las arterias se obstruyen por los depósitos de grasa y la placa, reduciendo el diámetro del torrente de sanguíneo y el flujo de la sangre.*

English Phrase	Spanish Phrase
One of the most important jobs of the blood is to carry oxygen to the tissues, muscles, and organs, including the heart itself.	*Una de las funciones más importantes de la sangre es llevar oxígeno a los tejidos, músculos, y órganos, incluyendo el corazón por mismo.*
If the arteries that supply oxygen to the muscle of the heart become narrowed, they may not supply enough oxygen for when the heart needs to beat rapidly (as during exercise).	*Si las arterias que suministran sangre al corazón se estrechan, es posible que no van a tener la capacidad a suministrar suficente oxígeno cuando el corazón tiene que golpear rápidamente (como durante el ejercicio).*
When the oxygen supply to the tissue is insufficient, it causes a painful condition called ischemia. Heart pain caused by ischemia is called angina.	*Cuando el suministro de oxígeno a los tejidos es insuficiente, causa una condición dolorosa que se llama isquemia. Dolor del corazón causado por isquemia se llama la angina.*
Sometimes a piece of fatty plaque may break off, causing a near-complete blockage of an artery. With no blood flow and no oxygen, the tissue supplied by the artery begins to die.	*A veces un pedazo de placa puede romper, causando una obstrucción total de una arteria. Sin flujo de sangre y sin oxígeno, el tejido suministrado por la arteria empieza a morir.*
When there is complete blockage of an artery of the heart, a heart attack occurs.	*Cuando hay una obstrucción total en una de las arterias del corazón, una parte del músculo del corazón muere, y se llama un ataque al corazón.*

English Phrase	Spanish Phrase
When there is complete blockage of an artery in the brain, it is called a stroke.	Cuando hay una obstrucción total en una de las arterias del cerebro, algunas de las células del cerebro mueren, y se llama un derrame cerebral.
Prevention of atherosclerosis helps to prevent heart attack and stroke.	La prevención de la aterosclerosis ayuda a prevenir el ataque al corazón y el derrame cerebral.
Fatty plaques that block the arteries are made of fats, cholesterol, and other substances.	Las placas que obstruyen las arterias son de grasas, el colesterol y otras sustancias.
Smoking and hypertension also contribute to atherosclerosis.	Fumando y la presión alta también contribuyen a la aterosclerosis.
Lowering the level of fats, or lipids, and the level of cholesterol in your bloodstream can help prevent atherosclerosis.	Reducir el nivel de grasas, o lípidos, y el nivel de colesterol en la sangre puede ayudar a prevenir la aterosclerosis.
Quitting smoking and controlling blood pressure are also important in preventing heart disease.	Dejar de fumar y controlar la presión arterial son también importantes en la prevención de enfermedades del corazón.
Diet and exercise can sometimes lower lipid and cholesterol levels, and control hypertension all by themselves.	La dieta y el ejercicio a veces pueden reducir el nivel de los lípidos, y el nivel de colesterol por mismos.

English Phrase	Spanish Phrase
Drugs are prescribed if diet and exercise are not enough.	*Medicamentos son recetados si la dieta y el ejercicio no son suficientes.*
Symptoms of a heart attack include: pressure, heaviness or pain in the chest, sometimes radiating to the arm, back, or jaw; shortness of breath; sweating, weakness, or dizziness; anxiety; and rapid or irregular heart beats.	*Los síntomas de un ataque al corazón incluyen: presión, pesado o dolor en el pecho, a veces moviendo al brazo, a la espalda, o a la mandíbula; dificultad respirando; sudor; debilidad o mareado; la ansiedad; y los latidos del corazón rápidos o irregulares.*
Symptoms of a heart attack last 30 minutes or longer and are not relieved by rest.	*Los síntomas del ataque al corazón duran a menos de treinta minutos, y no se desaparecen con descanso.*
Prompt treatment of a heart attack is important. If you think you are having a heart attack, don't wait; call 911.	*Tratamiento inmediato de un ataque al corazón es importante. Si usted piensa que tiene un ataque, no espere; llame a 911.*
Treatments for heart attack include oxygen, medications to break up clots blocking the arteries, pain medications, and drugs to improve heart function and circulation.	*Los tratamientos de un ataque al corazón incluyen el oxígeno, medicamentos para romper placas atascando las arterias, medicinas por dolor, y drogas para mejorar la función del corazón y de la circulación.*

English Phrase	Spanish Phrase
After a heart attack, surgery may be necessary to remove material blocking the arteries.	*Después de un ataque al corazón, cirugía puede ser necesaria para quitar las placas atascando las arterias.*

HYPERTENSION

English Phrase	Spanish Phrase
Normal blood pressure is less than 139/89. Hypertension is two or more blood pressures, measured at different times, above 140/90.	*La presión arterial normal es menos de 139/89. Presión alta es dos o más presiones, medidas a tiempos diferentes, más alta que 140/90.*
Hypertension can occur without symptoms.	*La presión alta puede ocurrir sin síntomas.*
Hypertension is one of the primary risk factors for heart disease and stroke.	*La presión alta es uno de los riesgos principales de los enfermedades del corazón y derrame cerebral.*
Hypertension can cause reduced blood flow to organs like the kidneys and eyes, affecting their function.	*La presión alta puede reducir el flujo de la sangre a los órganos como los riñones y los ojos, afectando su función.*
Hypertension can be improved by a healthy, low-salt diet, and regular exercise.	*La presión alta puede ser mejorada por una dieta saludable y baja en sal, y el ejercicio regular.*
Most often, drugs are prescribed to keep blood pressure at a normal level and prevent complications.	*La mayoría de las veces, medicamentos son prescritos para mantener la presión arterial en un nivel normal y prevenir complicaciones.*

SECTION 3

ILLNESSES

MIGRAINES

English Phrase	Spanish Phrase
Migraines are severe headaches characterized by throbbing or pulsing pain. They can last from four hours to several days.	*Las migrañas son dolores de cabeza muy intensos, caracterizados por dolor punzante. La migraña pueden durar cuatro horas a varios días.*
Migraine pain may be accompanied by nausea, vomiting, or sensitivity to light and sound.	*El dolor de las migrañas puede ser acompañado por la náusea, los vómitos, o sensitividad a la luz y los ruidos.*
Migraines can be so painful they interfere with daily activities.	*Las migrañas pueden ser tan dolorosas que impiden las actividades normales.*
Migraines may be triggered by foods, alcohol, emotional stress, the menstrual cycle, weather changes, and other factors in the environment.	*Las migrañas pueden ser causado por los alimentos, el alcohol, el estrés emocional, el ciclo de la menstruación, y otras cosas en el entorno.*
Occasional migraines can be treated with over-the-counter pain relievers like Tylenol.	*Las migrañas periódicas pueden ser tratado con medicinas como Tylenol, que se puede comprar a la farmacia.*
Frequent migraines (more than three a month) may require preventive medication.	*Las migrañas frecuentes (más que tres en una mes), pueden requerir medicamentos de prevención.*

SECTION 3

ILLNESSES

English Phrase	Spanish Phrase
Blood pressure medications, seizure medications, and anti-depressants are sometimes used to prevent migraines.	*Medicamentos para la presión arterial, para convulsiones, y antidepresivos están usado a veces para prevenir las migrañas.*

OBESITY

People who are overweight are at increased risk for many serious illnesses, including diabetes, heart disease, and arthritis.	*Las personas que tienen exceso de peso tienen más riesgo para muchas enfermedades graves, incluyendo la diabetes, la enfermedad del corazón, y la artritis.*
Weight loss by itself can reduce the severity of these conditions.	*Perder peso por mismo puede reducir la gravedad de estas condiciones.*
An effective weight loss plan should be based on a healthy, balanced diet that restricts the number of calories consumed daily.	*Un plan de peso pérdido debe incluir una dieta saludable que restricta el número de las calorias tomado cada día.*
Moderate exercise three or more times a week should be included in the weight loss plan.	*El ejercicio moderado tres o más veces cada semana debe ser una parte del plan de peso pérdido.*
It is important to plan for weight maintenance once the desired weight is reached. It is easy to return to old eating habits and regain weight that has been lost.	*Es importante tener un plan para mantener el peso cuando el peso deseado es alcanzado. Es fácil a volver a las costumbres malas y a recuperar el peso que ha sido perdido.*

English Phrase	Spanish Phrase
SHINGLES	
Adults who have had chicken pox as children may develop shingles (herpes zoster) when they are older.	*Los adultos que han tenido la varicela cuando eran niños pueden contraer el herpes cuando tienen más edad.*
The chicken pox virus stays dormant in the body and can be reactivated by stress, injury, or illness.	*El virus de varicela permanezca latente en el cuerpo y se reactiva por el estrés, la herida, o la enfermedad.*
Shingles appear as a rash in a band on one side of the body. The rash develops blisters and can be very painful. Sometimes, the rash spreads across the body.	*El herpes parecen por una erupción en una línea en un lado del cuerpo. La erupción contrae las ampollas y puede ser muy dolorosa. A veces, la erupción se extiende en el cuerpo.*
The rash usually lasts two to four weeks, and resolves by itself.	*Normalmente, la erupción dura dos a cuatro semanas, y se resuelve por mismo.*
The rash can affect the nervous system, so if you think you have shingles it is best to call your doctor.	*La erupción puede afectar el sistema nervioso, así que si piensa que tiene el herpes, es mejor llamar a su médico.*
Now there is a vaccine that can prevent shingles.	*Ahora hay una vacuna que puede prevenir el herpes.*

MEDICATIONS

This section isn't as long as some of the others, but that doesn't mean it's any less important. Getting a patient to take his or her medication correctly is no simple task. Hopefully, the following phrases will help you achieve this goal.

English Phrase	Spanish Phrase
INDICATIONS	
This medication is:	*Esta medicamento es:*
for pain	*para el dolor*
to control blood pressure	*para controlar la presión*
an antibiotic	*un antibiótico*
for depression	*para la depresión*
to prevent seizures	*para prevenir ataques*
to prevent the formation of blood clots	*para prevenir la formación de coágulos de sangre*
to control the blood sugar level	*para controlar el nivel de azúcar en la sangre*

English Phrase	Spanish Phrase
to control psychiatric symptoms	*para controlar los síntomas psiquiátricos*
for your cough	*para su tos*
for nasal congestion	*para la congestión nasal*
for heartburn/stomach pain	*para la acidez/dolor de estómago*
for chest pain	*para dolor del pecho*
to improve the function of the heart	*para mejorar la función del corazón*
to make breathing easier	*para hacer más fácil la respiración*
to prevent asthma	*para prevenir el asma*
to reduce inflammation	*para reducir la inflamación*
for constipation	*para el estreñimiento*
to help you sleep	*para ayudarle a dormir*

🎧 DOSAGE, ROUTINE, AND SCHEDULE

Take one/two/three pills once/twice/three times a day.

Tome una/dos/trés pastilla(s) una vez/dos veces/tres veces al día.

English Phrase	Spanish Phrase
Take one/two teaspoon(s) every four hours.	*Tome una/dos cucharadita(s) cada cuatro horas.*
Take the medicine before you go to bed.	*Tome la medicina antes de que se acueste.*
Take the medicine at the same time every day.	*Tome la medicina a la misma hora cada día.*
Take the medicine before meals.	*Tome la medicina antes de las comidas.*
Take the medicine every four/six/eight hours.	*Tome la medicina cada cuatro/seis/ocho horas.*
Continue to take the medication as directed for seven-ten days, or until it is all gone, even if you feel better.	*Siga tomando las medicinas según las indicaciones de siete/diez días, o hasta no hay más, aunque si se siente mejor.*
Do not stop taking the medication suddenly.	*No pare de tomar la medicina de repente.*
Draw up the medicine in a syringe, check that the dose is correct, and inject it into the fat under the skin of the belly or thigh.	*Saca la medicina en una jeringa, compruebe que la dosis es correcta, y inyecta la medicina bajo de la piel en la grasa de la panza o los muslos.*
Put one drop in each eye.	*Ponga una gota en cada ojo.*
Exhale, put the tube in the mouth, press the button, and inhale slowly.	*Exhale, ponga el tubo en la boca, apriete el botón y inhale lentamente.*

English Phrase	Spanish Phrase
Press the suppository gently into the rectum.	*Presione suavemente el supositorio en el recto.*

🎧 **PRN MEDICATIONS (AS NEEDED MEDICATIONS)**

English Phrase	Spanish Phrase
Take the medication only if you need it, but no more often than every two/four/six hours.	*Tome la medicina solamente si la necesita, pero no con más frecuencia que cada dos/cuatro/seis horas.*

🎧 **ALLERGIES**

English Phrase	Spanish Phrase
Do you have any drug allergies?	*¿Tiene alguna alergia a drogas?*
Signs of an allergic reaction include a rash, itching, mild fever, or aches in the muscles and joints.	*Los signos de una reacción alérgica incluyen una erupción, picazón, fiebre or dolores en los músculos y las articulaciones.*
Call 911 if you experience difficulty breathing, tightness in the chest, or swelling in the face, lips, tongue, or throat.	*Llame al 911 si usted experienca dificultad para respirar, opresión en el pecho, o hinchazón en la cara, labios, lengua, o garganta.*

🎧 **SIDE EFFECTS/PRECAUTIONS**

English Phrase	Spanish Phrase
Common side effects include:	*Efectos secundarios comunes incluyen:*
drowsiness	*la somnolencia*
dry mouth	*la sequedad de boca*

English Phrase	Spanish Phrase
nausea	*la náusea*
diarrhea	*la diarrea*
fatigue	*la fatiga*
headache	*el dolor de cabeza*
This medication may make you sleepy. You should not drive after taking it.	*Este medicamento puede producirle sueño. No debe manejar después de tomarla.*
This medication affects your body's ability to fight infection. You should wash your hands with care and avoid people who are sick.	*Este medicamento afecta la capacidad de su cuerpo para combatir infecciones. Debe lavarse las manos con cuidado y evitar las personas que están enfermas.*
This medication will make you bleed easily. You should use a soft toothbrush, avoid contact sports, and use an electric razor.	*Este medicamento le hará sangrar fácilmente. Debe usar un cepillo suave, evitar los deportes de contacto, y utilizar una rasuradora eléctrica.*
This medication can make your blood sugar dangerously low. You should always carry candy or juice, and take it if you feel weak, sweaty, or shaky.	*Este medicamento puede hacer el nivel de azúcar en su sangre peligrosamente bajo. Siempre debe llevar caramelos o jugo, y tómelo si se siente débil, inestable, o sudoroso.*

MEDICATIONS

English Phrase	Spanish Phrase
This medication can make you lightheaded or dizzy if you stand up too quickly.	*Esta medicina le puede hacer aturdido o mareado si usted se levanta rápidamente.*
You should wear a bracelet or carry a card to indicate you are taking this medication.	*Debe llevar una pulsera o llevar una tarjeta para indicar que usted está tomando esta medicina.*
Do not drink alcohol while taking this medication.	*No tome alcohol mientras toma este medicamento.*
Do not become pregnant while taking this medication. Use a good method of birth control.	*No se queda embarazada mientras toma este medicamento. Utiliza un método anticonceptivo bueno.*
Always tell your doctor or dentist you are taking this medication.	*Siempre digie a su doctor o su dentista que está tomando este medicamento.*
The medication will take two or three weeks to become effective.	*El medicamento tendrá dos o tres semanas para ser efectivo.*
Call your doctor if the medication is not working or if you feel worse.	Llame a su doctor si la medicina no funciona o si se siente peor.

X-RAYS, MRIs, AND OTHER MEDICAL TESTS

Of course, there are hundreds of different tests that could be ordered for a patient; we've focused on the most common. For some of the more obscure diagnostics, you can find phrases in this section that will be applicable for those as well.

English Phrase	Spanish Phrase
X-RAY	
What is your name?	¿Cómo se llama?
Please follow me.	Por favor, sígame.
You are here for an X-ray today?	¿Usted está aquí para una radiografía hoy?
Have you ever had an X-ray?	¿Alguna vez ha tenido una radiografía?
What part of your body are we taking an X-ray of today?	¿Qué parte de su cuerpo se toma una radiografía hoy?
¿Are you pregnant?	¿Está embarazada?
Is there a chance you could be pregnant?	¿Existe la posibilidad de que podría estar embarazada?
Please undress and put this gown on.	Por favor, desnudarse y ponerse este vestido.

MEDICAL TESTS

English Phrase	Spanish Phrase
You can leave your shoes and socks on.	*Usted puede dejar sus zapatos y calcetines.*
Please remove your socks and shoes.	*Por favor, elimine sus calcetines y zapatos.*
Please stand here.	*Por favor, párase aquí.*
Put your back against this board.	*Ponga la espalda en contra de esta placa.*
Stand here facing this board.	*Párase aquí frente a esta placa.*
Place your feet here.	*Coloque los pies aquí.*
Please stand very still and when I say so, take a breath and hold it.	*Por favor, quedarse muy quieto y cuando digo, tomar un respiro y sostenerla.*
Now breathe.	*Ahora respire.*
Place your arm here.	*Coloque el brazo aquí.*
Place your arm here with your palm up.	*Coloque el brazo aquí con la palma de la mano para arriba.*
Place your arm here with your palm down.	*Coloque el brazo aquí con la palma de la mano para abajo.*
Please do not move.	*Por favor, no se mueva.*

English Phrase	Spanish Phrase
Place your elbow here.	*Coloque el codo aquí.*
Place your hand here.	*Coloque la mano aquí.*
Place your hand here with your palm up.	*Coloque la mano aquí con la palma de la mano para arriba.*
Place your hand here with your palm down.	*Coloque la mano aquí con la palma de la mano hacia abajo.*
Please get up on this table.	*Póngase en esta mesa.*
Now lie down.	*Ahora se acueste.*
Please bend your leg.	*Por favor, doblar la pierna.*
Please keep your leg straight.	*Por favor, mantenga la pierna recta.*
MRI EXAM	
Have you ever had an MRI?	*¿Alguna vez ha tenido una resonancia magnética?*
When?	*¿Cuándo?*
Have you had any surgeries?	*¿Ha tenido alguna cirugía?*
When, and what type of surgery was it?	*¿Cuándo y qué tipo de cirugía fue?*

English Phrase	Spanish Phrase
Have you ever had radiation or chemotherapy treatment?	¿Alguna vez ha recibido radioterapia o quimioterapia?
Do you have a history of cancer?	¿Tiene usted historia de cáncer?
Do you have a history of diabetes?	¿Tiene usted historia de diabetes?
Do you have a history of high blood pressure?	¿Tiene usted historia de presión arterial alta?
Do you have a history of kidney problems?	¿Tiene usted historia de problemas renales?
Do you have a history of liver problems?	¿Tiene usted historia de problemas hepáticos?
Do you have a history of anemia?	¿Tiene usted historia de anemia?
Do you have a history of seizures?	¿Tiene usted historia de convulsiones?
Do you take prednisone or other steroid medication?	¿Toma usted la prednisona u otros medicamentos con esteroides?
Are you having any pain in the area that we are scanning today?	¿Tiene dolor en la zona de exploración que estamos haciendo hoy?
How bad is your pain on a scale of one to ten, ten being the worst pain you have ever had?	¿Tan malo es el dolor en una escala de uno a diez, siendo diez el peor dolor que usted ha tenido?

MEDICAL TESTS

English Phrase	Spanish Phrase
Do you have a pacemaker?	¿Tiene usted un marcapasos?
Do you have any implanted wires from your pacemaker?	¿Tiene alguna implantado cables del marcapasos?
Do you have an implanted insulin pump?	¿Tiene implantado una bomba de insulina?
Do you have an internal defibrillator for your heart?	¿Tiene usted un desfibrilador interno para el corazón?
Do you have a nerve stimulator in any part of your body?	¿Tiene un estimulador de nervios en cualquier parte de su cuerpo?
Have you ever had a stent placed in the arteries surrounding your heart?	¿Alguna vez ha colocado un stent en las arterias que rodean el corazón?
Do you have an implant in your eyes or ears?	¿Usted tiene un implante en los ojos o los oídos?
Have you ever had surgery for a brain aneurysm?	¿Alguna vez ha tenido un cirugía de aneurisma cerebral?
Do you have aneurysm clips inside your head?	¿Tiene aneurisma clips dentro de su cabeza?
Do you have any bullets or bullet fragments that remain inside your body?	¿Tiene alguna balas o fragmentos de bala que permanecen dentro de su cuerpo?
Have you ever had a heart valve replaced?	¿Usted ha tenido una válvula susistuida en el corazón?

English Phrase	Spanish Phrase
Do you have removable dental work?	¿Tiene usted trabajo dental removible?
Have you ever had rods, pins, plates, or screws placed in any part of your body?	¿Tiene alguna varas, planchuelas de chapa, o tornillos en cualquier parte de su cuerpo?
Have you ever had a joint replacement, such as your hip or knee?	¿Usted ha tenido un conjunto sustituye, como la cadera o la rodilla?
Are you wearing any patches on your body, such as a nicotine or nitroglycerin patch?	¿Está usted usando los parches de su cuerpo, como un parche de nicotina o nitroglicerina?
Have you ever done any welding or grinding work with sheet metal?	¿Alguna vez ha hecho alguno trabajo de soldadura o triturar con metal?
Have you ever had any metal pieces get under your skin or in your eye?	¿Alguna vez ha tenido alguna piezas de metal debajo de la piel o en el ojo?
When was your last menstrual period?	¿Cuándo fue su último período menstrual?
Are you pregnant?	¿Está embarazada?
Is there a chance you could be pregnant?	¿Existe la posibilidad de que podría estar embarazada?
Are you taking birth control or receiving hormone treatment?	¿Está tomando control de la natalidad o recibiendo tratamiento hormonal?

English Phrase	Spanish Phrase
Do you have any allergies to anything?	¿Tiene alguna alergia a algo?
Have you ever had dye injected into your vein during an X-ray?	¿Alguna vez ha tenido tinte inyecta en una vena durante una radiografía?
Have you ever had any kind of allergic reaction to the dye?	¿Alguna vez ha tenido una reacción alérgica a la tintura?
Are you afraid of being in small spaces?	¿Tiene miedo de estar en espacios pequeños?
The test will take about 15 (20) (30) minutes.	La prueba se llevará unos quince (veinte) (treinta) minutos.
Please hold very still during the test.	Por favor, mantenga muy quieto durante la prueba.
Please remove all jewelry and metal from your body.	Por favor, elimine todas las alhajas y metal de su cuerpo.

OTHER TESTS

BLOOD

I am going to draw your blood today.	Tengo que sacarle sangre hoy.
Please relax your arm.	Por favor, relaje el brazo.

English Phrase	Spanish Phrase
You can remove the bandage in 10 minutes.	*Usted puede retirar el vendaje en diez minutos.*
URINALYSIS/STOOL	
I need to get a urine sample from you.	*Tengo que obtener una muestra de su orina.*
I need a stool sample from you.	*Necesito una muestra de heces de usted.*
The restroom is here.	*El baño está aquí.*
Please use this container to collect your urine.	*Por favor, use este recipiente para recoger la orina.*
Please use this container to collect your stool.	*Por favor, use este recipiente para recoger sus heces.*
ECHOCARDIOGRAM	
Your doctor has ordered an echocardiogram.	*Su médico ha ordenado un ecocardiograma.*
An echocardiogram is an ultrasound of your heart.	*Un ecocardiograma es una prueba de ultrasonido de su corazón.*
It is a painless procedure.	*Es un procedimiento sin dolor.*
The test will tell your doctor some important information about your heart.	*La prueba le dirá a su médico información importante acerca de su corazón.*

English Phrase	Spanish Phrase
ELECTROCARDIOGRAM	
Your doctor has ordered an EKG.	*Su médico ha ordenado un electrocardiograma de su corazón.*
I will be placing electrodes on your chest and stomach for the test.	*Voy a colocar los electrodos en el pecho y el estómago para la prueba.*
The test will help your doctor identify abnormalities in your heart.	*La prueba ayudará a su médico a identificar anomalías en su corazón.*
CT SCAN	
Your doctor has ordered a test called a CT scan.	*Su médico ha ordenado una prueba llamada tomografía computadorizada.*
It is similar to an X-ray, but is more precise.	*Es similar a una radiografía, pero es más precisa.*
You will lie on a table and the machine will move around you taking pictures.	*Se recostará en una mesa y la máquina se mueva a su alrededor tomando fotos.*
You will have dye injected into your vein for the test.	*Usted tendrá tinte inyectado en una vena para la prueba.*

English Phrase	Spanish Phrase
You must remove all jewelry and/or metals from your body.	*Usted debe quitar todas las joyas y los metales de su cuerpo.*
You must hold very still during the test.	*Usted no debe moverse durante la prueba.*

SECTION 3

MEDICAL TESTS

OBSTETRICS AND GYNECOLOGY

Mothers usually put their children first; so let's start this section that way as well.

English Phrase	Spanish Phrase
LABOR AND DELIVERY	
Why are you here today?	¿Por qué está usted aquí hoy?
Are you having contractions?	¿Tiene contracciones?
Is there any bleeding?	¿Está sangrando?
Has your water broken?	¿Ha roto la bolsa de agua?
Is your baby moving normally?	¿Mueve su bebe normalmente?
When is your due date?	¿Cuándo es su fecha para dar la luz?
Is this your first baby?	¿Es su primer bebé?
How many children do you have?	¿Cuantos hijos tiene usted?
In what year was your first child born? Your second? Your third?	¿En cuál año nació su primero hijo? ¿Su segundo? ¿Su tercero?

English Phrase	Spanish Phrase
Were all your babies full term? Were any of your babies premature?	¿Todos de sus hijos nacieron a nueve meses? ¿Fueron algunos de sus hijos prematuros?
How many weeks pregnant were you when they were born?	¿Cuántas semanas del embarazo tenía usted cuando nacieron?
Did you have diabetes or high blood pressure with any of your pregnancies? Were there any other complications?	¿Tuvo diabetes o presión alta con algun de sus embarazos? ¿Habían otras complicaciones?
Have you had any caesarean sections?	¿Ha tenido algunas cesáreas?
Have you had any problems with this pregnancy?	¿Ha tenido problemas o complicaciones con este embarazo?
Who is your doctor?/Which is your clinic?	¿Quién es su doctor?/¿Cuál es su clínica?
Do you plan to use medication for pain?	¿Está planeando usar una medicina por dolor?
Do you prefer IV sedation or an epidural?	¿Prefiere medicina en el suero o el bloque peridural?
Here is a hospital gown. Please change your clothes.	Aquí está una bata. Por favor, cambie su ropa.
I need a urine specimen, please. There is the bathroom.	Necesito una espécimen de orina, por favor. Aquí está el baño.

English Phrase	Spanish Phrase
Please lie down and I will examine you.	*Acuéstese, por favor; voy a examinarle.*
MEDICAL HISTORY	
Do you have any health problems?	*¿Tiene usted problemas de salud?*
Are you taking any medications?	*¿Está tomando algun medicamentos?*
Do you have any allergies?	*¿Tiene alguna alergias?*
Do you have a history of:	*¿Tiene usted un historia de:*
heart problems?	*problemas del corazón?*
high blood pressure?	*presión alta?*
lung problems like tuberculosis or asthma?	*problemas con los pulmones como tuberculosis o asma?*
diabetes?	*diabetes?*
kidney problems or urinary tract infections?	*problemas con los riñones o infecciones orinarias?*
thyroid problems?	*problemas con los tiroides?*
problems with the bones and joints like arthritis?	*problemas con los huesos o los artículos como artritis?*

English Phrase	Spanish Phrase
problems with the liver like hepatitis?	*problemas con el hígado como hepatitis?*
problems with menstruation, or with the uterus or ovaries?	*problemas con la menstruación, o con la matrice o las ovarias?*
sexually transmitted diseases?	*infecciones sexuales?*
depression or other psychological problems?	*depresión or otros problemas psicológicos?*
seizures, migraines, or other problems of the nervous system?	*ataques, migrañas, o otros problemas del sistema nervioso?*
drug or alcohol abuse?	*abuso de drogas o alcohol?*
Do you smoke?	*¿Fuma usted?*
Have you had any surgeries?	*¿Ha tenido algunas cirugías?*
When and for what condition?	*¿Cuándo y para qué condición?*
Have you ever been hospitalized for an illness or an accident?	*¿Ha sido hospitalizada por una enfermedad o un accidente?*
Have you ever had anesthesia?	*¿Ha tenido anestesia?*

English Phrase	Spanish Phrase
Will you accept a blood transfusion if there is an emergency?	¿Va a aceptar una transfusión de sangre si hay una emergencia?
I am going to draw some blood for laboratory studies.	Voy a sacar sangre por estudios de laboratorio.
I am going to check your cervix now.	Voy a examinar la boca de matrice ahora.
Please bend your knees and put your feet together.	Por favor, doble las rodillas y ponga los pies juntos.
Open the legs, please.	Abra las piernas, por favor.
Your cervix is dilated 8 centimeters.	Su boca de matrice está dilatado ocho centimetros.
Everything is progressing normally.	Todo progresa normalmente.
The baby will be born soon.	El bebé va a nacer pronto.
It will be a while yet.	Será un rato aún.
There is a problem, and we recommend your baby be delivered by caesarean section.	Hay un problema, y recomendamos que su parto sea por cesárea.
The baby is breech, and you will need a caesarean section.	El bebé esta parada, y necesita una cesárea.
You are fully dilated and it is time to push.	La boca de matrice está dilatada completa y es la hora a empujar.

English Phrase	Spanish Phrase
Push!	¡Empuje!
Don't push now.	No empuje ahora.
Pull your legs back, hold your breath, and push while I count to 10.	Jale sus piernas, mantenga la respiración, y empuje mientras yo cuento hasta diez.
That's it!	¡Así!
The baby is coming.	Ya viene el bebé.
It's a boy/girl!	¡Es un niño/una niña!
POSTPARTUM	
You will need some stitches.	Necesita algunos puntos de sutura.
The doctor is going to repair the laceration.	La doctora va a reparar la laceración.
I am going to check that your uterus is firm and your bleeding normal.	Voy a asegurar que la matrice está firme y sangradura normal.
Do you have any pain?	¿Tiene algún dolor?
Where does it hurt?	¿Dónde le duele?
Would you like some medicine for the pain?	¿Le gustaría alguna medicina para el dolor?

English Phrase	Spanish Phrase
BREASTFEEDING	
Would you like to feed the baby now?	*¿Le gustaría a dar pecho a su bebé ahora?*
You can give him the right side for 15 to 30 minutes, then give him the left side, if he wants.	*Puede darle el lado derecho por quince a treinta minutos, y después le dé el izquierdo, si él lo quiere.*
The milk supply usually comes in on the third day after the birth.	*La leche materna normalmente viene el tercer día después del nacimiento.*
Feed your baby whenever she acts hungry, and let her eat until she is full.	*Alimente a su bebé cada vez que ella parece como tiene hambre, y la deje comer hasta que está llena.*
It is normal for newborns to feed 8 to 12 times a day.	*Es normal que los recién nacidos comen ocho a doce veces al día.*
OFFICE VISIT	
How old were you when you had your first period?	*¿A qué edad tuvo su primera menstruación?*
Are your periods regular?	*¿Su menstruación es regular?*
Are you sexually active?	*¿Usted está teniendo relaciones sexuales?*
What do you use for birth control?	*¿Qué usa usted para anticonceptivo?*

SECTION 3

OB/GYN

English Phrase	Spanish Phrase
It is important to use condoms to protect yourself from sexually transmitted disease.	*Es importante a utilizar condones para protegerse de las enfermedades sexuales.*
I would like to do a speculum exam now.	*Me gustaría hacer un examen del espéculo ahora.*
I will do a pap smear, and take samples to check for sexually transmitted diseases.	*Voy a hacer un examen pap, y voy a tomar espécimen para buscar infecciones sexuales.*
Please try to relax.	*Por favor, trate de relajarse.*
I will do a manual exam now.	*Voy a examinarle con las manos ahora.*
I am going to examine your breasts now.	*Voy a examinar sus senos ahora.*
Your pap smear was abnormal.	*Su prueba de papanícolaou fue anormal.*
We will need to do a more definitive exam, called a colposcopy, to check your cervix for cancer.	*Necesitamos hacer una prueba más definitiva, que se llama una colposcopia, para buscar su boca de matrice por cáncer.*

BIRTH CONTROL

What would you like to use for birth control?	*¿Qué le gustaría utilizar para control de la natalidad?*

English Phrase	Spanish Phrase
The most effective methods of birth control are sterilization and the IUD.	*Los métodos más efectivos de control de natalidad son la esterilización y el dispositivo intrauterino.*
Birth control pills and shots are about 98 percent effective.	*Las píldoras anticonceptivas y la inyeccíon son cerca de noventa y ocho por ciento efectivos.*
Condoms, the diaphragm, and the rhythm method are less effective, but can work if used correctly.	*Los condones, el diafragma, y los métodos naturales son menos efectivos, pero pueden funcionar si se usan correctamente.*

PEDIATRICS: BASICS

The section covering pediatrics will be presented in two parts. In this section, we'll cover basic statements regarding a patient's history, such as their household environment (living conditions, diet, exercise) and so forth. The second part of the pediatrics section will cover statements regarding common childhood ailments.

English Phrase	Spanish Phrase
HISTORY	
Why are you here today?	*¿Por qué está usted aquí hoy?*
What is your relationship to the child?	*¿Cuál es su relación al niño?*
How long has he/she had these symptoms?	*¿Cuánto tiempo ha tenido él/ella estos síntomas?*
Has he/she had these symptoms before? When?	*¿Ha tenido él/ella estos síntomas antes? ¿Cuándo?*
Has he/she been treated for the symptoms?	*¿Ha tenido él/ella tratamiento por estos síntomas?*
Was the treatment effective?	*¿Fue el tratamiento efectivo?*

English Phrase	Spanish Phrase
Tell me about illnesses the child has had in the past.	*Dígame acerca de las enfermedades que el niño ha tenido en el pasado.*
Has he/she ever been hospitalized?	*¿Ha sido él/ella hospitalizado alguna vez?*
Has he/she ever had surgery?	*¿Ha tenido él/ella alguna cirugía?*
For what condition?	*¿Por cuál condición?*
When did this occur?	*¿Cuándo ocurrió esto?*
Is he/she currently taking any medications?	*¿Está él/ella tomando algunos medicamentos ahora?*
Does he/she have any allergies?	*¿Tiene él/ella alergias?*
Does he/she have other health problems?	*¿Tiene él/ella otros problemas de salud?*
Do you have a record of his/her vaccinations?	*¿Tiene un recuerdo de sus vacunas?*
Did you (did his mother) have any problems during pregnancy?	*¿Tuvo usted (tuvo su mamá) algunos problemas durante el embarazo?*
Did you (did his mother) take any drugs, smoke, or drink alcohol during the pregnancy?	*¿Durante el embarazo, tomó usted (su mamá) algunas drogas, fumó, o tomó alcohol?*

English Phrase	Spanish Phrase
How many weeks pregnant were you (was her mother) when he/she was born?	¿A cuántas semanas del embarazo nació él/ella?
Was it a vaginal or caesarean delivery?	¿Fue un nacimiento vaginal o por cesárea?
Did the child have any problems immediately after birth?	¿Tuvo el niño problemas inmediamente después del nacimiento?
How much did the child weigh?	¿Cuánto pesó?
How long was he/she in the hospital after delivery?	¿Cuánto tiempo estaba él/ella en el hospital después del parto?
Was he/she breastfed or bottlefed?	¿Fue alimentado con biberón o por el pecho?
At what age were solid foods introduced?	¿A qué edad se introdujo alimentos sólidos?
At what age did he/she first sit alone? Walk? Talk?	¿A qué edad se sentó solo? ¿Anduvo? ¿Habló?
At was age was he/she potty trained?	¿A qué edad se le bañó solo?
Does he/she attend daycare?	¿Va él/ella a la guardería?
What does the child do during an average day?	¿Qué hace el niño durante un día usualmente?
How is he/she doing in school?	¿Cómo está en la escuela?

English Phrase	Spanish Phrase
Tell me about his/her household. Who does he/she live with?	*Dígame acerca de su hogar. ¿Con quién vive él/ella?*
Where does he/she live?	*¿Dónde vive él/ella?*
Are there any major health problems in the family?	*¿Hay algunos problemas de salud importantes en la familia?*
Does he/she have siblings? Are they healthy?	*¿Tiene él/ella hermanos? ¿Están saludables?*
How is his/her appetite?	*¿Cómo es su apetito?*
Tell me about his/her diet.	*Dígame acerca de su dieta.*
How many hours does the child sleep at night?	*¿Cuántas horas duerme el niño de noche?*
Does he/she have nightmares or other sleep disturbances?	*¿Tiene él/ella pesadillas u otros trastornos del sueño?*
Are there any behavior problems that concern you?	*¿Hay algunos problemas de conducta que le preocupa?*
SAFETY EDUCATION	
Always put the child to sleep on her back.	*Siempre ponga su bebé a dormir acostado en su espalda.*

English Phrase	Spanish Phrase
Keep the crib free of pillows, extra blankets, and toys.	*Mantenga la cuna libre de almohadas, mantas extras, y juguetes.*
Never shake a baby.	*Nunca sacuda a un bebé.*
Move sharp or dangerous objects up out of the baby's reach.	*Mueve objetos afilados o peligrosos fuera del alcance del bebé.*
Move medicines, cleaning supplies, and chemicals up out of the baby's reach, or buy devices to babyproof cabinets.	*Mueve medicinas, cosas de limpieza, y productos químicos fuera del alcance del bebé, o compre dispositivos para prevenir que el bebé entre en los gabinetes.*
Block electrical outlets.	*Bloque de tomas eléctricas.*
Buy gates to keep the child off the stairs and out of rooms that are not safe.	*Compre puertas a guardar el niño fuera de las escaleras y de los cuartos que no están seguros.*
Always place the child in a carseat when traveling by car.	*Siempre ponga al niño en un asiento de seguridad cuando viaja en un coche.*
The safest place in the car is in the middle of the back seat.	*El lugar más seguro en el coche está en el centro del asiento trasero.*
Never leave the child alone in the bath.	*Nunca deje al niño solo en la bañera.*

English Phrase	Spanish Phrase
Talk to your doctor before giving medicines to your child. Doses for children are not the same as for adults.	*Hable con su doctor antes de darle las medicinas a su hijo. Las dosis para niños no son iguales que las por los adultos.*
Teach the child not to talk to strangers.	*Enseñe al niño a no hablar con extraños.*
Teach the child your name, address, and telephone number.	*Enseñe al niño su nombre, su dirección, y su número de teléfono.*
Teach the child that it is important to tell a trusted adult if anyone touches him/her in a way that makes him/her uncomfortable.	*Enseñe al niño que es importante decir a un adulto de confianza si alguien le toca a él/ella en una manera que le hace incómodo.*
Make a family escape plan in case of fire. Teach the child what to do.	*Haga un plan de fuga para la familia en caso de incendio. Enseñe al niño lo que hacer.*
Teach the child how to walk on the sidewalk and to cross the street safely.	*Enseñe al niño como caminar en la acera y a cruzar la calle con seguridad.*
Make sure your child wears a safety helmet when riding a bicycle.	*Asegúrese que se ponga un casco de seguridad mientras está montado en una bicicleta.*
Teach the child never to go in or near the water unless an adult is present.	*Enseñe al niño que nunca debe entrar en o cerca del agua, a menos que un adulto esté presente.*

SECTION 3

PEDIATRICS

English Phrase	Spanish Phrase
Talk to your child about alcohol, tobacco, and drugs.	*Hable con su hijo acerca de alcohol, tabaco, y drogas.*
Talk to your child, or ask the doctor or nurse to talk to your child, about safe sex and the prevention of sexually transmitted diseases.	*Hable con su hijo, o pregúntale a su doctor o enfermera que habla con su hijo acerca del sexo seguro y la prevención de las enfermedades sexuales.*
Teach your child never to handle guns unless an adult is present.	*Enseñe a su niño que nunca debe manejar las armas a menos que un adulto esté presente.*

DIET AND EXERCISE

English Phrase	Spanish Phrase
Feed the baby whenever he/she shows signs of hunger.	*Alimente al bebé cada vez que muestra señas de hambre.*
It is normal for babies to eat every two to three hours, or eight to 12 times in a 24-hour period.	*Es normal que los bebés comen cada dos a tres horas, o ocho a doce veces en veinticuatro horas.*
Feed the baby only formula or breastmilk. The baby does not need water or juice.	*Alimente al bebé solamente fórmula o leche materna. El bebé no necesita agua ni jugo.*
Introduce soft foods when the child is six months old. Rice cereal is a good first food.	*Empieze alimentos sólidos cuando el bebé tiene seis meses. Cereal de arroz es un buen primer alimento.*
Introduce new foods one at a time, until you see how your baby reacts to it.	*Introduzca nuevos alimentos de uno en uno, hasta que vea como reacciona su bebé a los nuevos alimentos.*

English Phrase	Spanish Phrase
Do not give the baby strawberries or honey until he/she is one year old.	*No le dé al bebé miel o fresas hasta que él/ella tenga un año de edad.*
Give your toddler two cups of whole milk or yogurt or cheese every day.	*Dé a su niño dos tazas de leche entera, queso, o yogurt cada día.*
Offer your toddler a wide variety of healthy foods, including grains and cereals, meat, fish and beans, and fruits and vegetables every week.	*Ofrezca a su hijo una amplia variedad de alimentos saludables, incluidos panes y cereales, carne, pescado y frijoles, frutas y vegetales cada semana.*
Encourage your child to play outdoors each day.	*Anime a su hijo a jugar afuera cada día.*

SECTION 3

PEDIATRICS

COMMON CHILDHOOD ILLNESSES

Here are phrases associated with some of the more common childhood ailments. Some of these phrases can be found in the section entitled "Illnesses" as well.

English Phrase	Spanish Phrase
ADHD	
Attention deficit hyperactivity disorder (ADHD) is one of the most common behavioral problems of childhood.	*El trastorno de déficit de atención con hiperactividad (TDAH) es uno de los problemas de comportamiento más comunes de la infancia.*
Children with ADHD have trouble concentrating, are easily distracted, and are over-active and impulsive.	*Los niños con TDAH tienen dificultad para concentrarse, se distraen fácilmente, y son demasiado activos y impulsivos.*
Their behavior may become a problem at home or at school.	*Su comportamiento puede llegar a ser un problema en la casa o en la escuela.*
A child is diagnosed with ADHD when other problems that might cause the behaviors are ruled out.	*Un niño se diagnostica con TDAH después de otras condiciones que pudieran causar las conductas están excluidas.*

English Phrase	Spanish Phrase
Medications are sometimes prescribed to help improve the child's concentration.	*Medicamentos son recetados a veces para ayudar a mejorar la concentración del niño.*
Parents can also learn how to help their child to discipline himself and to succeed in school and in other activities.	*Los padres también pueden aprender cómo ayudara su hijo a disciplinarse y a tener éxito en la escuela y otras actividades.*

ASTHMA

Asthma is a disease of the airway of the lungs. During an attack, the airways constrict and produce mucus, making the passage of air in and out of the lungs difficult.	*El asma es una enfermedad de las vías respiratorias en los pulmones. Durante un ataque, las vías respiratorias contraen y producen una mucosa, haciendo la entrada y salida del aire en los pulmones difícil.*
Symptoms of asthma include wheezing, shortness of breath, pressure in the chest and a cough, especially at night or early in the morning.	*Los síntomas del asma incluyen la sibilancia, falta del aire, la presión en el pecho, y tos, especialmente en la noche o temprano en la mañana.*
Asthma is a chronic condition, but attacks usually occur only occasionally.	*La condición del asma es crónica, pero los ataques ocurren solamente periódicamente.*
An asthma attack is often triggered by exposure to allergens such as pollen or tobacco smoke.	*Un ataque del asma puede ser causado cuando el paciente es expuesto a agentes environmentales, como polen o humo del tabaco.*

English Phrase	Spanish Phrase
An asthma attack may be triggered by exercise or stress, or by illness like cold or flu.	*Un ataque del asma puede ser causado de ejercicio físico, de estrés, o de enfermedades como la gripa o la influenza.*
You can control asthma symptoms by taking anti-inflammatory medications prescribed by your doctor on a regular basis.	*Se puede controlar los síntomas del asma para tomando medicamentos contra la inflamada recetados de su doctor regularmente.*
You can relieve an asthma attack by using an inhaled medication prescribed by your doctor when symptoms occur.	*Se puede aliviar un ataque del asma utilizando medicamento inhalado, recetado de su doctor, cuando los síntomas ocurren.*
If medications are not working and you continue to have difficulty breathing, you must call your doctor or go to the emergency room.	*Si los medicamentos no funcionen, y se continúa a tener dificultad respirando, debe llamar su doctor o ir a la sala de urgencias.*

CANDIDIASIS

Anyone can get a yeast infection, but they are common in children who are nursing and who are still in diapers.	*Cualquier persona puede sufrir una infección por levaduras, pero son comunes en los niños que están tomando el pecho y que están en pañales.*

English Phrase	Spanish Phrase
A yeast infection in the mouth looks like white patches over the interior cheeks, gums, and tongue.	*Una infección por levaduras en la boca parece como manchas blancas sobre los cachetes interiores, las encías, y la lengua.*
A yeast infection in the diaper area appears as a rash of little red dots over reddened skin.	*Una infección por levaduras en la área de los pañales parece como una erupción de pequeños puntos rojos en la piel roja.*
Yeast in the mouth can be painful and may make it difficult for a child to eat. Be sure they are taking enough breastmilk or formula to avoid dehydration.	*Una infección por levaduras en la boca puede ser dolorosa, y a veces es difícil para el niño comer. Asegúrese que está tomando suficiente leche materna o fórmula para evitar la deshidratación.*
Treat yeast in the mouth with Nystatin, which you can buy at the pharmacy. Follow the directions on the package.	*Trate una infección por levaduras en la boca con Nystatin, que se puede comprar en la farmacia. Siga las instrucciones en el paquete.*
If you are breastfeeding, you should have your breasts checked for yeast.	*Si usted está amamantando, debe tener su pecho buscar por una infección por levaduras.*

CHILDHOOD ILLNESSES

English Phrase	Spanish Phrase
Treat diaper rash infections with clotrimazole cream, which you can also buy at the pharmacy. You may want to see the pediatrician to make sure the rash is caused by yeast.	*Trate una infección por levaduras en la área del pañal con la crema clotrimazole, que se puede comprar en la farmacia. Si lo desea, puede ver el doctor para confirmar de que la erupción es causada por la levadura.*
Yeast infections should clear up within seven days after beginning treatment.	*Las infecciones por levaduras deben aclararse dentro de los siete días de comenzar el tratamiento.*

CHICKEN POX

Chicken pox is a common illness among children less than 12 years of age.	*La varicela es una enfermedad común, especialmente entre los niños menores de doce años de edad.*
Symptoms of chicken pox include a rash of itchy blisters that usually start on the chest, back, or face and spread to the entire body.	*Los síntomas de la varicela incluyen una erupción de ampollas con picor que generalmente empiezan en el pecho, la cara, o la espalda, y se extiende a todo el cuerpo.*
The rash may spread to the genitals and inside the nose and mouth.	*La erupción puede extenderse a los genitales y al dentro de la boca y la nariz.*
The rash is normally accompanied by flu-like symptoms.	*La erupción normalmente está acompañado con síntomas como la gripa.*

English Phrase	Spanish Phrase
The rash lasts one to two weeks and clears up without treatment.	*La erupción dura una a dos semanas y se aclara sin tratamiento.*
Chicken pox is very contagious, so children who are sick should not go to school or play with other children until symptoms are gone.	*La varicela es muy contagiosa, y los niños con la enfermedad no deben ir a la escuela o jugar con otros niños hasta los síntomas desaparecen.*
A vaccination for chicken pox is recommended at age 18 months, and again at four to six years.	*Una vacuna contra la varicela es recomendado a la edad de diez y ocho meses, y otra vez a cuatro a seis años de edad.*
Healthy children who have already had the chicken pox are immune and do not need the vaccine.	*Los niños saludables que ya han tenido la varicela son inmunes, y no necesitan la vacuna.*
A child who has had the vaccine may still develop a mild case of chicken pox.	*Un niño que ha tenido la vacuna todavía puede desarrollar un caso leve de la varicela.*
CROUP	
Croup is a condition caused by several viral infections that cause inflammation of the upper airway.	*Crup es una enfermedad producida por varias infecciones virales que causan la inflamación de las vías respiratorias.*

CHILDHOOD ILLNESSES

English Phrase	Spanish Phrase
The most typical croup symptom is a cough that sounds like the barking of a seal.	*El síntoma más típico de crup es una tos que suena como el ladrido de una foca.*
The child may also make a squeaking sound on exhalation.	*El niño también puede hacer un sonido de chirrían con la exhalación.*
Croup usually resolves without treatment.	*Crup usualmente se resuelve sin tratamiento.*
You can treat the cough and help the child breathe more comfortably by having the child breathe moist air. Use a humidifier or sit with the child in a steamy bathroom with the door closed and the hot water running.	*Se puede tratar la tos, y ayudar el niño a respirar más fácilmente por hacer que respire aire húmedo. Use un humidificador o siéntese con el niño en un baño de vapor con la puerta cerrada y el agua caliente corriendo.*
Sometimes the airways become so inflamed that the child does not get enough oxygen. If your child is blue around the mouth or is using the muscles around the ribs and collarbones to breathe, he needs immediate medical attention.	*A veces las vías respiratorias son tan inflamadas que el niño no obtiene suficiente de oxígeno. Si su hijo parece azul acerca de la boca, o usa los músculos alrededor de las costillas y los huesos del cuello para respirar, él necesita atención medical inmediamente.*

FEVER

Fever is a common symptom of many illnesses, most of them mild.	*La fiebre es un síntoma común de muchas enfermedades, la mayoría leves.*

SECTION 3

CHILDHOOD ILLNESSE

English Phrase	Spanish Phrase
Fever in a young child should be evaluated very carefully. When in doubt, see your pediatrician.	La fiebre en un niño pequeño debe ser evaluada con mucho cuidado. Cuando hay duda visite su pediatra.
To treat fever from a mild illness, give Tylenol or Motrin—never aspirin. Baths in tepid (not cold) water will help to bring a high fever down.	Para tratar la fiebre de una enfermedad leve use Tylenol o Motrin—nunca aspirina. Los baños con agua tibia ayudan para reducir la fiebre.
Always consult a doctor or nurse for the right dosage of Tylenol for a child less than two years of age.	Siempre consulte con su médico o su enfermera para la dosis correcta para los niños menos de dos años de edad.
High fever can cause seizures in young children. Seizures should be reported to the doctor.	La fiebre alta puede causar convulsiones en los niños pequeños. Debe informar su médico de las convulsiones.

GROUP A STREP

Group A strep is the bacteria that causes strep throat.	Estreptococo grupo A es una bacteria que causa la garganta por estreptococos.
A child with strep will have a high fever, a sore throat, and will appear very ill.	Un niño con el estreptococo tendrá una fiebre alta, el dolor de garganta, y parecerá muy enfermo.
The strep bacteria releases a toxin into the blood that causes scarlet fever and can damage the heart and other organs.	La bacteria streptococa libera una toxina en la sangre que causa la escarlatina y que puede causar daño al corazón y otros órganos.

SECTION 3

CHILDHOOD ILLNESSES

English Phrase	Spanish Phrase
Suspected group A strep infections should always be treated with antibiotics.	*Las infecciones posibles estreptococo deben ser tratadas siempre con antibióticos.*

GROUP B STREP

English Phrase	Spanish Phrase
Group B strep is another form of the strep bacteria that can cause fatal infections in newborns.	*Estreptococo grupo B es otra forma de la bacteria streptococa que puede causar infecciones fatales in los recién nacidos.*
Group B strep is carried on the skin, where it is very common and does not cause problems.	*Estreptococo grupo B se lleva en la piel, donde es muy común y donde no causa problemas.*
If a pregnant woman carries the bacteria on her genitals, the bacteria can enter the infant's body through the eyes, nose or mouth, and he/she can become seriously ill.	*Si una mujer embarazada lleva la bacteria en sus genitales, la bacteria puede entrar al cuerpo del bebé por los ojos, la nariz, o la boca, y él/ella puede verse gravemente enfermo.*
Pregnant women are tested for group B strep before their delivery, and are given penicillin while in labor if they carry the bacteria.	*Las mujeres embarazadas son pruebadas por el estreptococo grupo B antes del parto, y le dan penicilina si ellas llevan la bacteria.*
Penicillin given to the mother helps to prevent infection in the newborn.	*Dándole la penicilina a la madre ayuda a prevenir infección en el recién nacido.*

English Phrase	Spanish Phrase
JAUNDICE	
Jaundice is a condition that affects newborns in the first few days of life.	*La ictería es una condición que afecta los recién nacidos en los primeros días de vida.*
Jaundice can occur when the blood type of the baby is different from that of the mother.	*La ictería puede ocurrir cuando el tipo de sangre del bebé es diferente de la madre.*
The difference in blood types causes greater than normal destruction of blood cells in the baby.	*La diferencia en los tipos de sangre causa más destrucción que normal en los células rojos en el bebé.*
The newborn's liver is immature, and cannot eliminate all the waste products from the destroyed cells.	*El hígado del bebé recién nacido es inmaturo, y no puede eliminar todos los productos de desecho de los células destruidos.*
The waste products, called bilirubin, collect in the baby's body, causing the skin to turn yellow.	*Los productos de desecho, llamado la bilirrubina, colectan en el cuerpo del bebé, causando la piel a parecer amarilla.*
If the level of bilirubin in the body becomes very high, it can cause brain damage.	*Si el nivel de la bilirrubina es muy alta, se puede causar daño al cerebro.*
Light helps to break down bilirubin so it can be eliminated from the body in the stool.	*La luz ayuda a romper la bilirrubina hasta pueda ser eliminado en las heces.*

English Phrase	Spanish Phrase
The therapy for jaundice is to put the baby under lights and to monitor the level of bilirubin until it starts to decline. This can take two or three days.	*La terapia por la ictería es poner el bebé debajo de la luz y vigilar el nivel de la bilirrubina hasta que el nivel empieza a decaer. Esto puede tomar dos o tres días.*

MENINGITIS

Meningitis is a viral or bacterial infection of the fluid in the spine and brain.	*La meningitis es una infección viral o bacterial de la fluida de la espina y el cerebro.*
Viral meningitis is serious, but usually resolves without complications. Bacterial meningitis can be fatal.	*La meningitis viral es grave, pero usualmente se resuelve sin complicaciones. La meningitis bacterial puede ser fatal.*
If you suspect your child has meningitis, see a doctor right away.	*Si sospecha que su hijo tiene meningitis, consulte con su médico inmediatamente.*
Symptoms of meningitis include headache, high fever, and stiff neck. There may be vomiting, sensitivity to light, confusion, and sleepiness.	*Los síntomas de la meningitis incluyen dolor de cabeza, fiebre alta, y rigidez en el cuello. Puede haber vómitos, sensibilidad a la luz, confusión y somnolencia.*
Children under age 2 may only appear slow or inactive, or cry more than usual, or eat poorly.	*Niños menos de dos años pueden parecer más inactivos, o llorar más que normal, o comer mal.*
Children of any age may have seizures.	*Los niños de cualquier edad pueden tener las convulsiones.*

English Phrase	Spanish Phrase
Treatment of bacterial meningitis is antibiotics, and these should be started as early as possible to prevent death.	*El tratamiento de la meningitis bacterial incluye los antibióticos, que deben ser comenzado tan pronto como sea posible para evitar la muerte.*
Treatment of viral meningitis is supportive: fluids, rest, Tylenol for pain and fever.	*El tratamiento de la meningitis viral es suportivo: líquidos, descanso, Tylenol para el dolor y la fiebre.*

OTITIS MEDIA

Ear infections are probably the most common illness among young children.	*Las infecciones de los oídos probablemente son las enfermedades más comunes en los niños pequeños.*
Ear infections should always be evaluated by the doctor, and treated if necessary, because untreated infections can cause hearing damage.	*Las infecciones de los oídos siempre deben ser evaluadas por un médico, y tratadas si es necesario, porque las infecciones que no se tratan pueden causar las lesiones auditivas.*
It is sometimes difficult to detect ear infections, because the most common symptom—pain in the ear—cannot be reported by children too young to speak.	*A veces es difícil a percibir las infecciones de los oídos, porque el síntoma más común—el dolor en el oído—no puede ser contado por los niños jovencitos que no pueden hablar.*

English Phrase	Spanish Phrase
Irritability, poor appetite, fever, pulling at the ears, or not responding normally to sounds may be signs that a baby has an ear infection.	*La irritabilidad, el apetito mal, la fiebre, jaliendo los oídos, o no reaccionando normalmente a los ruidos pueden ser signos que un bebé tiene una infección en los oídos.*

RSV

English Phrase	Spanish Phrase
Respiratory syntactical virus (RSV) is an upper respiratory infection that can be serious in young children.	*El virus sintáctico respiratorio (VSR) es una infección respiratoria que puede ser grave en los niños pequeños.*
RSV season is fall and winter.	*La temporada para el VSR es el otoño y el invierno.*
Symptoms are similar to those of the common cold, sometimes with fever. Infants may simply appear lethargic, with poor appetite.	*Los síntomas parecen similares al resfrío, a veces con fiebre. Los bebés pueden parecer apáticos o irritables, con el apetito mal.*
Some infections may become serious enough that children, especially infants, do not receive enough oxygen.	*Algunas infecciones pueden ser suficientemente graves que los niños, especialmente los bebés, no reciben suficiente oxígeno.*
A young child with rapid respirations, retractions (visible use of the muscles of the ribs and collarbones to breathe), and a blue color around the mouth may need to be hospitalized for oxygen therapy.	*Un bebé con respiraciones rápidas, retracciones (uso visible de los músculos de las costillas y los huesos del cuello para respirar), y un color azul cerca de los labios pueden necesitar ser hospitalizada para terapia del oxígeno.*

English Phrase	Spanish Phrase
VACCINATIONS	
All children should be vaccinated against a variety of contagious viral and bacterial diseases.	*Todos los niños deben ser vacunado contra varias enfermedades infecciosas virales y bacteriales.*
Vaccinations are the single most important thing you can do to protect the health of both your child and your community.	*La vacuna es la cosa más importante que usted puede hacer a protegir la salud de su hijo y su comunidad.*
Many public schools will not admit children who have not been vaccinated.	*Muchas escuelas públicas no dejan pasar a los niños que no han sido vacunados.*
There is little evidence that vaccines cause autism, as has been reported in the media.	*No hay evidencia significativa que las vacunas causan el autismo, como lo que ha sido reportado por los medios de comunicación.*
Most pediatricians strongly believe that the benefits of vaccination far outweigh the risks.	*La mayoría de las pediatras creen firmemente que los beneficios superan a los riesgos.*
There are several new vaccinations available in the past five years that are now recommended for children.	*Hay varias vacunas nuevas disponibles en los pasados cinco años que ahora están recomendadas para los niños.*

CHILDHOOD ILLNESSES

English Phrase	Spanish Phrase
The Centers for Disease Control and Prevention (CDC) has an excellent website in Spanish that provides the complete vaccination schedules for children and teens. Your pediatrician will also have a schedule.	*El centro para control y prevenir de enfermedades tiene una página de la Web excelente en español que da el programa completo para los niños y los adolescentes. Su pediatra también tiene un programa.*
You should maintain a record of your child's vaccinations that you keep at home.	*Debe mantener un archivo de las vacunas de su hijo en su casa.*

SECTION 3

CHILDHOOD ILLNESSE

ELDER CARE

The section on elder care will provide you with useful phrases when working with this population. Remember, certain members of this population may not be alert to person, place, or time, and additional changes/disruptions in their environment can increase this sense of confusion. Be patient and, when needed, use a family member to gather the information.

English Phrase	Spanish Phrase
COMMON PHRASES	
Do you wear dentures?	*¿Utiliza dentaduras?*
Are they partial or full dentures?	*¿Utiliza dentaduras parciales o completas?*
Do you have problems chewing or swallowing?	*¿Tiene problemas masticando o tragando?*
How much fluids do you drink a day?	*¿Cuánto líquido toma al día?*
Are you able to cook?	*¿Puede cocinar?*
How many meals do you eat a day?	*¿Cuántas veces come al día?*

ELDER CARE

English Phrase	Spanish Phrase
Do you have nausea/vomiting?	*¿Tiene náusea o vómito?*
Have you lost weight unintentionally?	*¿Ha perdido peso sin tratar?*
Do you wear glasses?	*¿Utiliza lentes?*
Are the glasses bifocals?	*¿Los lentes son bifocales?*
Do you wear contact lenses?	*¿Utiliza lentes de contacto?*
Do you drive?	*¿Usted maneja?*
Do you have a valid driver's license?	*¿Tiene una licencia válida para conducir?*
Do you have/wear a medical alert bracelet?	*¿Tiene o utiliza una pulsera de alerta médica?*
Have often do you have a bowel movement?	*¿Qué tan seguido defeca?*
Do you have urinary or bowel incontinence?	*¿Tiene incontinencia orinaria o en defecación?*
Do you have constipation?	*¿Tiene estreñimiento?*
Do you have diarrhea?	*¿Tiene diarrea?*
Do you get up to urinate at night? If so, how often?	*¿Se levanta en la noche para orinar? Si, sí, qué tan seguido?*

English Phrase	Spanish Phrase
PATIENT'S HISTORY	
Do you exercise?	¿Hace ejercicio?
Are you single/married/divorced/widowed?	¿Es soltero/casado/divorciado/viudo?
Do you live alone?	¿Vive solo/a?
If not, who do you live with?	¿Si no, con quién vive?
Do you own or rent your home?	¿Es dueño de o renta su casa?
Do you have medical insurance, Medicare, Medicaid, or disability?	¿Tiene seguro médico, Medicare, Medicaid, o incapacidad?
Do you have a pension?	¿Tiene una pensión?
What is your financial situation?	¿Cuál es su situación financiera?
Do you live in a one-story or two-story home?	¿Vive un una casa de un piso o dos pisos?
Do you engage in social activities?	¿Participa en actividades sociales?
Are you able to do your finances/pay bills?	¿Puede manejar sus finanzas/hacer pagos?
Do you have a good support system?	¿Tiene un buen sistema de apoyo?

SECTION 3

ELDER CARE

English Phrase	Spanish Phrase
Are you close to your family?	¿Es cercano a su familia?
Are you sexually active?	¿Es sexualmente activo?
If yes, do you use protection?	¿Si sí, utiliza protección?
Do you feel depressed/hopeless/anxious?	¿Se siente deprimido/sin ánimos/ansioso/a?
Do you have thoughts of hurting yourself?	¿Tiene pensamientos de lastimarse a si mismo?
Do you smoke? If yes, how much and for how long?	¿Fuma? ¿Si sí, cuánto y por cuánto tiempo?
Do you drink? If yes, how much and what type?	¿Bebe alcohol? ¿Si sí, cuánto y qué tipo de alcohol?

PINPOINTING THE PROBLEM

Do you have musculoskeletal pain/stiffness?	¿Tiene dolor/rigidez músculo esqueletar?
Do you have numbness/tingling in your extremities?	¿Tiene hormigueo/calambres en sus extremidades?
Do you have loss of coordination?	¿Tiene pérdida de coordinación?
Do you have an unsteady gait?	¿Su andar es desequilibrado?
Do you have chronic pain?	¿Tiene dolor crónico?
Do you use a cane?	¿Utiliza un bastón?

English Phrase	Spanish Phrase
Do you use a walker?	*¿Utiliza una andadera para caminar?*
Do you use a wheelchair?	*¿Utiliza un silla de ruedas?*
Have you had any recent falls?	*¿Ha tenido caídas recientemente?*
Have you had any loss of consciousness recently?	*¿Ha perdido el conocimiento/desmayado recientemente?*
Are you able to complete your activities of daily living?	*¿Puede llevar sus actividades diarias sin problemas?*
Are you hard of hearing?	*¿Tiene problemas para oír?*
Do you wear hearing aids?	*¿Utiliza audífonos para escuchar?*
Do you use unilateral or bilateral hearing aids?	*¿Utiliza un audífono o dos audífonos para escuchar?*
Do you take daily medications?	*¿Toma medicamentos diarios?*
Do you take a daily multivitamin?	*¿Toma vitaminas diarias?*
Do you take daily calcium?	*¿Toma calcio diario?*
When was your last bone density test?	*¿Cuándo fue su último examen para medir la densidad de sus huesos?*
When was your last colonoscopy?	*¿Cuándo fue su última colonoscopia?*

English Phrase	Spanish Phrase
When was your last mammogram?	*¿Cuándo fue su último mamograma?*
When was your last prostate exam?	*¿Cuándo fue su último examen de la próstata?*
When was your last blood test to check for prostate specific anigen (PSA)?	*¿Cuándo fue su último examen de sangre de la próstata?*
When was your last pelvic exam/Pap smear?	*¿Cuándo fue su último examen pélvico/cervical/Papanicolau?*

MENTAL HEALTH

Do you know what day/month/year it is?	*¿Sabe qué día/mes/año es?*
Do you have a hard time remembering things?	*¿Tiene dificultades para recordar cosas?*
Do you have problems remembering what pills to take and when to take them?	*¿Tiene problemas para recordar cuáles pastillas tomar y cuándo tomarlas?*
Do you have a family history of Alzheimer's?	*¿Su familia tiene historia de Alzheimer's?*
I am going to perform a balance test (Romberg's): Close your eyes and stand with your feet together.	*Voy a hacerle un examen para probar su balance (Romberg's): Cierre los ojos y párese con los pies juntos.*
I am going to perform a mini mental exam.	*Voy a hacerle un pequeño examen mental.*
I am going to check your reflexes.	*Voy a revisarle los reflejos.*

English Phrase	Spanish Phrase
Do you have insomnia?	¿Tiene insomnio/dificultad para dormir?
Have many hours do you sleep daily?	¿Cuántas horas duerme al día?

PHYSICAL THERAPY

The movement questions are at the end of this section, but before jumping to that point, we begin with some basic queries to help you gain a clearer idea of the patient's physical health.

English Phrase	Spanish Phrase
INTRODUCTION	
Hello. My name is...	*Hola. Mi nombre es* (your name).
We are going to be doing some physical therapy today.	*Vamos a hacer terapia física hoy.*
Physical therapy will help you get back to your normal activities.	*La terapia física le ayudará a volver a sus actividades normales.*
Physical therapy will help improve your flexibility and strength.	*La terapia física ayudará a mejorar su flexibilidad y fuerza.*
During the first session, I will be asking you a series of questions.	*Durante el primer período de sesiones, le pediré a usted una serie de preguntas.*
Let's begin.	*Empecemos.*

English Phrase	Spanish Phrase
GATHERING INFORMATION	
Presently, what is your chief complaint?	*¿Actualmente, cuál es su queja principal?*
What is your usual occupation?	*¿Cuál es su ocupación habitual?*
How long have you done that type of work?	*¿Cuánto tiempo ha usted hecho ese tipo de trabajo?*
Are you able to work right now?	*¿Es usted capaz de trabajar ahora mismo?*
Are you able to enjoy your regular hobbies or other activities?	*¿Es usted capaz de disfrutar sus aficiones regulares o otras actividades?*
Have you recently had surgery?	*¿Ha tenido recientemente una cirugía?*
What kind of your surgery did you have?	*¿Qué tipo de cirugía tuvo?*
When was the surgery?	*¿Cuándo fue la cirugía?*
Were there complications from the surgery?	*¿Hubo complicaciones de la cirugía?*
Have you done any type of activity since your surgery?	*¿Ha hecho algún tipo de actividad desde su cirugía?*
Did you have an injury?	*¿Tuvo una lesión?*
How were you injured?	*¿Cómo se lesionó?*

PHYSICAL THERAPY

English Phrase	Spanish Phrase
When was your injury?	*¿Cuándo fue su lesión?*
Have you done any type of activity since your injury?	*¿Ha hecho algún tipo de actividad desde su lesión?*
Do you have a history of diabetes?	*¿Tiene usted historia de diabetes?*
Do you have a history of cancer?	*¿Tiene usted historia de cáncer?*
Do you have a history of high blood pressure?	*¿Tiene usted historia de presión arterial alta?*
Do you have a history of arthritis?	*¿Tiene usted historia de artritis?*
Do you have a history of heart problems?	*¿Tiene usted historia de problemas del corazón?*
Do you have a history of lung problems?	*¿Tiene usted historia de problemas pulmonares?*
Do you have a history of osteoporosis?	*¿Tiene usted historia de osteoporosis?*
Have you had any prior surgeries?	*¿Ha tenido alguna cirugía antes?*
When?	*¿Cuándo?*
Do you have any other medical conditions that I should know about?	*¿Tiene alguna otra condición médica que yo debería saber?*
Are you taking any medications?	*¿Está tomando algún medicamento?*

English Phrase	Spanish Phrase
What are they?	*¿Qué son?*
Do you have any allergies?	*¿Tiene alguna alergia?*

PAIN

English Phrase	Spanish Phrase
Are you in pain?	*¿Tiene dolor?*
Where is your pain?	*¿Dónde está su dolor?*
On a scale of one to ten, ten being the worst pain you have ever felt, how bad is your pain?	*¿En una escala de uno a diez, siendo diez el peor dolor que usted ha tenido, qué tan grave es su dolor?*
Is your pain constant or does it come and go?	*¿Su dolor es constante o se va y viene?*
Is your pain sharp? Dull?	*¿Su dolor es fuerte? ¿Sordo?*
What makes your pain worse?	*¿Qué hace su dolor empeorar?*
What relieves your pain?	*¿Qué alivia su dolor?*
Are you taking pain medication?	*¿Está tomando algún medicamento para el dolor?*
If you are taking pain medication, you should take it before having physical therapy.	*Si está tomando medicamento para el dolor, usted debe tomarlo antes de la terapia física.*

PHYSICAL THERAPY

English Phrase	Spanish Phrase
PINPOINTING THE PROBLEM	
Do you have stiffness? Swelling?	*¿Tiene la rigidez? ¿Hinchazón?*
Where?	*¿Dónde?*
Prior to your surgery/injury, were you able to walk without assistance?	*¿Antes de su cirugía/lesión, fue capaz de caminar sin ayuda?*
When you walk, do you become short of breath?	*Cuando usted camina, ¿se queda corto de aliento?*
How far can you walk before you become short of breath?	*¿Hasta qué punto se puede caminar antes de quedar corto de aliento?*
If you did not walk on your own, did you use a cane? A walker? Crutches? A wheelchair?	*¿Si no caminaba por su propia cuenta, usaba un bastón? ¿Un andador? ¿Muletas? ¿Una silla de ruedas?*
Do you have difficulty dressing yourself?	*¿Tiene usted dificultad para vestirse?*
Do you have difficulty washing your hair?	*¿Tiene usted dificultad para lavar su cabello?*
Do you have difficulty brushing your teeth?	*¿Tiene usted dificultad para cepillarse los dientes?*
Do you have difficulty feeding yourself?	*¿Tiene usted dificultad para comer?*
Do you have difficulty going up or down stairs?	*¿Tiene usted dificultad para subir o bajar escaleras?*

English Phrase	Spanish Phrase
Do you have difficulty walking?	¿Tiene dificultad para caminar?
Do you have difficulty lifting?	¿Tiene usted dificultad para levantar?
Do you have difficulty throwing?	¿Tiene usted dificultad para tirar?
Do you have difficulty kneeling?	¿Tiene dificultad rodillándose?
Do you have problems sleeping?	¿Tiene problemas para dormir?
Do you have difficulty sitting for long periods of time?	¿Tiene usted dificultad para sentarse durante largos períodos de tiempo?
Do you have difficulty standing for long periods of time?	¿Tiene dificultad de pie durante largos períodos?
Do you have difficulty bending over?	¿Tiene usted dificultad para agacharse?
Do you have difficulty with any other activity that I have not mentioned?	¿Tiene dificultad con cualquier otra actividad que no he mencionado?
Do you feel your condition is getting better? Worse? Staying the same?	¿Usted cree que su condición está mejorando? ¿Peor? ¿Mantener el mismo?
MOVEMENT TEST	
I am going to ask you to do a series of movements.	Voy a pedirle que haga una serie de movimientos.

English Phrase	Spanish Phrase
If at any time you feel pain, let me know.	*Si en algún momento usted siente el dolor, hágamelo saber.*
Touch your chin to your chest.	*Tocar la barbilla al pecho.*
Move your head from side to side.	*Mueva la cabeza de lado a lado.*
Please stand up.	*Por favor, de pie.*
Now, try to balance yourself on one leg.	*Ahora, tratar de equilibrar en una pierna.*
Walk forward a few steps.	*Caminar hacia adelante.*
Now stop.	*Ahora para.*
Bend over and touch your feet.	*Doblarse y toca los pies.*
Stand up and twist from side to side.	*De pie y girar de lado a lado.*
Bend at the waist from side to side.	*Doblar a la cintura de un lado a otro.*
Please sit down.	*Por favor, siéntese.*
Touch your shoulders to your ears.	*Toque los hombros a los oídos.*
Rotate your shoulders forward in a circular motion	*Gire los hombros hacia delante en un movimiento circular.*

English Phrase	Spanish Phrase
Rotate your shoulders backward in a circular motion.	*Gire los hombros hacia atrás en un movimiento circular*
Extend your right arm.	*Amplíe el brazo derecho.*
Bend your right arm at the elbow.	*Doble el brazo derecho en el codo.*
Extend your left arm.	*Amplíe el brazo izquierdo.*
Bend your left arm at the elbow.	*Doble el brazo izquierdo en el codo.*
With both arms, reach for the ceiling.	*Con ambos brazos, alcance el techo.*
Bend your fingers.	*Doble los dedos.*
Extend your fingers.	*Amplíe los dedos.*
Flex your wrists.	*Extenda las muñecas.*
Extend your wrists.	*Amplíe las muñecas.*
Bend your right knee. Left knee.	*Doble la rodilla derecha. Rodilla izquierda.*
Extend your right knee. Left knee.	*Amplíe la rodilla derecha. Rodilla izquierda.*
Straighten your right knee. Left knee.	*Enderece la rodilla derecha. Rodilla izquierda.*
Point your toes up toward the ceiling.	*Punte los dedos del pie hacia el techo.*

English Phrase	Spanish Phrase
Point your toes downward.	*Punte los dedos del pie hacia abajo.*
Move your feet in circles to the right. To the left.	*Mueva los pies en círculos a la derecha. A la izquierda.*
We are now finished with your initial evaluation.	*Ahora estamos terminado con su evaluación inicial.*

DENTISTRY

While most people do not go to the dentist unless they absolutely have to, when they get there, they want to be understood.

English Phrase	Spanish Phrase
GENERAL STATEMENTS	
Why are you here today?	*¿Por qué está aquí hoy?*
How long has it been since you've seen a dentist?	*¿Cuánto tiempo ha sido desde que ha visto a un dentista?*
You should see a dentist two times per year.	*Usted debe ver a un dentista dos veces al año.*
When was the last time you had your teeth cleaned?	*¿Cuándo fue la última vez que se ha limpiado los dientes?*
You should have your teeth cleaned two times per year.	*Usted debería haber limpiado los dientes dos veces al año.*
How often do you brush your teeth?	*¿Con qué frecuencia se cepilla los dientes?*

English Phrase	Spanish Phrase
You should brush your teeth at least twice per day.	*Usted debe cepillarse los dientes al menos dos veces por día.*
You should use a soft bristled toothbrush and toothpaste that contains fluoride.	*Debe usar una cerda suave cepillo de dientes y dentífrico con flúor.*
Do you floss your teeth?	*¿Limpia con seda dental?*
You should floss your teeth at least once a day.	*Usted debe usar seda dental al menos una vez al día.*
Regular checkups can help you prevent gum disease.	*Los chequeos regulares le puede ayudar a prevenir la enfermedad de las encías.*
Symptoms of gum disease include red gums, sore and swollen gums, bleeding gums, loose teeth, sensitive teeth and bad breath.	*Los síntomas de la enfermedad de las encías son las encías rojas, hinchadas y dolor en las encías, sangrado de encías, dientes sueltos, sensibilidad dental y mal aliento.*

BEFORE THE EXAM

We will be examining your teeth today and checking for gum disease.	*Vamos a examinar hoy los dientes y el control de la enfermedad de las encías.*
Do you have any allergies to any medications? Food? Latex? The environment?	*¿Tiene alguna alergia a algún medicamento? ¿Alimentos? ¿Látex? ¿Medio ambiente?*

English Phrase	Spanish Phrase
Do you have any current medical problems?	*¿Tiene algún problema médico actual?*
(OR) Are there any changes in your health since your last visit?	*¿Hay algún cambio en su salud desde su última visita?*
Tell me about your past medical problems.	*Hábleme de sus pasados problemas médicos.*
Do you have anemia?	*¿Tiene usted anemia?*
Do you have problems with your blood clotting?	*¿Tiene problemas con la coagulación de la sangre?*
Are you diabetic?	*¿Es diabético?*
Do you have heart disease?	*¿Tiene enfermedad del corazón?*
Do you have lung disease?	*¿Tiene enfermedad pulmonar?*
Do you have osteoporosis?	*¿Tiene usted osteoporosis?*
Do you have hepatitis, HIV, or AIDS?	*¿Tiene hepatitis, HIV, o SIDA?*
Do you smoke or chew tobacco?	*¿Fuma o mastica tabaco?*
Do you drink alcohol?	*¿Bebe alcohol?*
How much? How often?	*¿Cuánto? ¿Con qué frecuencia?*

English Phrase	Spanish Phrase
Are you pregnant?	¿Está usted embarazada?
Is there a chance you could be pregnant?	¿Existe la posibilidad de que podría estar embarazada?
Are you planning to get pregnant?	¿Está planeando un embarazo?
Are you taking any medications?	¿Está tomando algún medicamento?
(OR) Are there any medication changes since your last visit?	¿Hay algún cambio en los medicamentos desde su última visita?
Are you taking aspirin? Coumadin? Plavix? Lovenox?	¿Está tomando aspirina? ¿Coumadín? ¿Plavix? ¿Lovenox?
Do you take a multivitamin every day?	¿Toma una multivitamina todos los días?
PAIN	
Are you having any pain?	¿Tiene algún dolor?
Where is your pain?	¿Dónde está su dolor?
On a scale of one to ten, ten being the worst pain you ever had, how bad is your pain?	¿En una escala de uno a diez, siendo diez el peor dolor que usted ha tenido siempre, qué tan malo es su dolor?

English Phrase	Spanish Phrase
How long have you been having this pain?	¿Cuánto tiempo lleva con este dolor?
What makes the pain worse?	¿Qué hace que el dolor empeore?
What makes your pain better?	¿Qué hace que el dolor mejore?
Are your teeth sensitive to cold? Heat?	¿Son sus dientes sensibles al frío? ¿Calor?
Does it hurt when you bite down?	¿Le duele cuando muerda?
Does it hurt when you open your mouth wide?	¿Le duele cuando abre la boca amplia?
X-RAYS	
When was the last time you had x-rays of your teeth?	¿Cuándo fue la vez última que usted tuvo radiografías de sus dientes?
I am going to be taking x-rays today.	Voy a tomar radiografías hoy.
I will be placing this lead apron over you for your protection.	Colocaré este delantal del plomo sobre usted para su protección.
Open your mouth.	Abra la boca, por favor.
Bite down on this.	Muerde esto.

DENTISTRY

English Phrase	Spanish Phrase
Please don't move.	*Por favor, no se mueva.*
Take a breath and hold it.	*Tome un respiro y sosténgalo.*
Now breathe.	*Ahora respire.*
Open your mouth.	*Abra la boca.*

EXAM/CLEANING

I am going to examine your teeth now.	*Voy a examinar ahora sus dientes.*
(Or) I am going to clean your teeth now.	*Voy a limpiar los dientes ahora.*
Please open your mouth wide.	*Por favor, abra su boca más amplia.*
A little wider, please.	*Un poco más amplio, por favor.*
Please tell me if anything I do causes you pain.	*Por favor, dígame si hay algo que causa dolor.*
I am going to check for gum disease.	*Voy a buscar la enfermedad de las encías.*
I am going to poke each tooth to check for cavities.	*Voy a meter cada diente para ver si hay caries.*
I am going to rinse your mouth.	*Voy a aclarar su boca.*
Gargle with this.	*Haga gárgaras con ésta.*

DENTISTRY

English Phrase	Spanish Phrase
Spit it out here.	*Escupe a cabo aquí.*
You have:	*Usted tiene:*
a cavity.	*caries.*
two cavities.	*dos caries.*
three cavities.	*tres caries.*
four cavities.	*cuatro caries.*
I am going to give you an injection with novacaine to numb your mouth.	*Voy a darle una inyección de novacaine para adormecer la boca.*
Just try to relax.	*Intente relajarse.*
Take a deep breath.	*Tome una respiración profunda.*
Once your mouth is numb, I will fill your cavities.	*Una vez que su boca esté adormecida, voy a llenar su caries.*
Is your mouth numb yet?	*Está la boca adormecida aún?*
Tell me if you have any pain while I am filling your cavities.	*Dime si tiene dolor, mientras hago la fijación de sus caries.*
Wait until the novacaine wears off before you eat.	*Espere que el novacaine desaparece antes de comer.*

PSYCH EVALUATION

We've included brief versions of mental health exams at other sections of the phrase book; that same basic exam is at the end of this section, but the rest of the section is devoted to other areas of common mental illnesses.

English Phrase	Spanish Phrase
BASIC INFORMATION	
What is the reason you are here today?	¿Cuál es la razón por la que está aquí hoy?
How old are you?	¿Cuántos años tiene?
Are you married? Single? Widowed? Divorced?	¿Es usted casado? ¿Único? ¿Viudo? ¿Divorciado?
Do you have any medical problems?	¿Tiene algún problema médico?
Have you ever been hospitalized for psychiatric problems?	¿Alguna vez ha sido hospitalizado por problemas psiquiátricos?
Why were you hospitalized?	¿Por qué fue hospitalizado?
¿When were you hospitalized?	¿Cuándo fue hospitalizado?

English Phrase	Spanish Phrase
For how long were you hospitalized?	*¿Cuánto tiempo estuvo hospitalizado?*
Do you feel that hospitalization helped you? Why? Why not?	*¿Cree usted que la hospitalización lo ayudó? ¿Por qué? ¿Por qué no?*
Have you ever been in an outpatient psychiatric program?	*¿Ha estado alguna vez en un programa ambulatorio psiquiátrico?*
When did you participate in an outpatient program?	*¿Cuándo participó en un programa ambulatorio?*
How long was the program?	*¿Cuánto tiempo fue el programa?*
Do you feel that the outpatient program helped you? Why? Why not?	*¿Cree usted que el programa ambulatorio lo ayudó? ¿Por qué? ¿Por qué no?*
Do you have any allergies to any medication? Foods? Latex?	*¿Tiene alguna alergia a algún medicamento? ¿Alimentos? ¿Látex?*
What are your current medications?	*¿Cuáles son sus medicamentos corrientes?*
Do you usually take your medications as prescribed?	*¿Suele tomar sus medicamentos, según lo estipulado?*
Do you ever miss a dose? Why?	*¿Usted olvida una dosis? ¿Por qué?*
Are you having any bothersome side effects from your medications?	*¿Tiene alguna molestos efectos secundarios de sus medicamentos?*

English Phrase	Spanish Phrase
What type of side effects are you having?	*¿Qué tipo de efectos secundarios?*

FRIENDS AND FAMILY

Do you live alone? Or with others?	*¿Vive solo? ¿O con otros?*
Who do you live with?	*¿Con quién vive?*
Do you have a support system?	*¿Tiene un sistema de apoyo?*
Who is among your support system?	*¿Quién está entre su sistema de apoyo?*
Are both your parents still alive?	*¿Son vivos sus padres?*
Do you have any brothers and sisters?	*¿Tienes hermanos y hermanas?*
Are you close to anyone in your family?	*¿Está usted cerca de alguien en su familia?*
Do you have problems getting along with members of your family?	*¿Tiene problemas para llevarse bien con los miembros de su familia?*
Do you have a lot of friends?	*¿Tiene muchos amigos?*
Do you have problems getting along with your friends?	*¿Tiene problemas para llevarse bien con sus amigos?*
Do you have children? How many?	*¿Tiene hijos? ¿Cuántos?*

English Phrase	Spanish Phrase
How old are your children?	¿Qué edad tienen sus hijos?
Do you have problems getting along with your children?	¿Tiene problemas para llevarse bien con sus hijos?
Do you have a lot of ups and downs in your relationships?	¿Tiene un montón de altibajos en sus relaciones?
What is your occupation?	¿Cuál es su ocupación?
Are you currently off work? Working?	¿Está usted actualmente libre del trabajo? ¿Trabaja?
How many jobs have you had in the last five years?	¿Cuántos empleos ha tenido en los últimos cinco años?
Are you having problems with your relationships at work?	¿Tiene problemas con sus relaciones en el trabajo?
Have you ever had a drinking problem?	¿Alguna vez ha tenido un problema con el alcohol?
When was your last drink?	¿Cuándo fue el último trago?
What other types of recreational drugs do you use?	¿Qué otros tipos de drogas recreativas usa?
Do you have a problem with prescription drugs?	¿Tiene usted un problema con los medicamentos recetados?

English Phrase	Spanish Phrase
Have you ever been in a drug or alcohol treatment program?	*¿Ha estado alguna vez en un programa de tratamiento de drogas o alcohol?*
MOOD/SLEEP DISORDERS	
Are you depressed?	*¿Está usted deprimido?*
How has depression affected your life?	*¿Cómo ha afectado su vida la depresión?*
Have you stopped doing the things that you used to enjoy?	*¿Ha dejado de hacer las cosas que solía disfrutar?*
When was the last time you remember not being depressed?	*¿Cuándo fue la última vez que recuerda no estar deprimido?*
Do you ever feel hopeless? Helpless?	*¿Usted se siente sin esperanza? ¿Desamparado?*
Are you a nervous person?	*¿Es usted una persona nerviosa?*
Do you ever have panic attacks?	*¿Alguna vez ha tenido ataques de pánico?*
Do you anger easily?	*¿Se enoja con facilidad?*
Are you easily irritated?	*¿Es usted irritado fácilmente?*
Do you sleep too much?	*¿Duerme demasiado?*

English Phrase	Spanish Phrase
Do you have trouble sleeping?	¿Tiene problemas para dormir?
Do you have trouble falling asleep?	¿Batalla usted para poder dormir?
Do you have trouble staying asleep?	¿Tiene problemas para quedarse dormido?
Do you wake up early in the morning before being fully rested?	¿Usted se despierta por la mañana temprano, antes de ser plenamente descansado?
Has your mood affected your appetite?	¿Ha afectado su estado de ánimo a su apetito?
Do you eat too much? Too little?	¿Usted come demasiado? ¿Muy poco?
Have you ever thought about harming yourself?	¿Alguna vez ha pensado en perjudicar a si mismo?
What kind of ways have you thought about to harm yourself?	¿Qué tipo de medios ha pensado en dañar a si mismo?
Have you ever tried to harm yourself?	¿Alguna vez ha intentado perjudicar a si mismo?
How long ago?	¿Cuánto tiempo hace?
Have you ever thought about harming someone else?	¿Alguna vez ha pensado en perjudicar a otra persona?
Have you ever tried to harm someone else?	¿Alguna vez ha tratado de dañar a otra persona?
When?	¿Cuándo?

English Phrase	Spanish Phrase
Do you have a plan for harming yourself now?	¿Tiene usted un plan para dañar a si mismo ahora?
Do you have a plan for harming someone else?	¿Tiene usted un plan para dañar a otra persona?
When you're feeling bad, do you ever cut or mutilate yourself?	¿Cuando se siente mal, piensa en cortar o mutilar a si mismo?

EATING DISORDERS

Have you ever felt like you were overweight?	¿Alguna vez usted se sentía sobrepeso?
Have you ever taken laxatives to keep from gaining weight?	¿Alguna vez ha tomado laxantes para evitar subir de peso?
Have you ever made yourself vomit to keep from gaining weight?	¿Alguna vez ha hecho provoque el vómito para evitar subir de peso?
Do you ever go on eating binges?	¿Alguna vez continúa usted a comer borracheras?

COMPULSION/DELUSIONS

Do you ever do things like washing your hands repeatedly, or checking things over and over, to make sure they are done properly?	¿Alguna vez hace las cosas como lavarse las manos repetidas veces, o comprobar las cosas una y otra vez, para asegurarse de que estén hechas correctamente?
Have people been harassing you lately?	¿Alguien lo haestado molestando?

English Phrase	Spanish Phrase
Have people been trying to harm you?	*¿Alguien ha tratado hacerle daño?*
Do you ever hear voices?	*¿Usted oye voces?*
What do the voices tell you to do?	*¿Qué dicen las voces?*
Do the voices ever tell you to hurt yourself?	*¿Dicen las voces que haga daño a si mismo?*
Do the voices ever tell you to hurt someone else?	*¿Las voces nunca le dicen que haga daño a alguien?*
Do you ever see things that you don't think are real?	*¿Usted ve las cosas que no cree que son reales?*
Do you ever smell things that other people don't smell?	*¿Alguna vez huele cosas que otras personas no huelen?*
Do you ever get a funny taste inside your mouth?	*¿Ha tenido algún sabor extraño en la boca?*
Do you feel as if your thoughts are racing?	*¿Se siente como si sus ideas son corriendo?*
Do you have frequent mood changes?	*¿Tiene frecuentes cambios de humor?*
Do you ever feel full of energy and extremely happy?	*¿Usted se siente lleno de energía y muy feliz?*
How long do these periods last?	*¿Cuánto tiempo dura todo eso?*
During these periods, do you ever do things you regret, like having unprotected sex, or spending too much money?	*Durante estos períodos, ¿hace usted cosas que lamentar, como tener relaciones sexuales sin protección, o gastar demasiado dinero?*

English Phrase	Spanish Phrase
Do you ever feel empty inside?	*¿Alguna vez se siente vacío?*
Do you have problems really knowing who you are?	*¿Tiene problemas realmente sabiendo quién es usted?*

BASIC MENTAL HEALTH EXAM

Can you tell me the date today?	*¿Me puede decir la fecha de hoy?*
Can you tell me where we are right now?	*¿Me puede decir dónde estamos ahora?*
Please repeat these words: tree - sofa - yellow.	*Por favor, repita estas palabras: árbol - sofá - amarillo.*
Please remember these words as I will ask you to recall them later.	*Por favor, recuerde estas palabras que yo le voy a recorder despues.*
Who is the President of the United States?	*¿Quién es El Presidente de los Estados Unidos?*
When is your birthday?	*¿Cuándo es su cumpleaños?*
When is your spouse's birthday?	*¿Cuándo es el cumpleaños de su cónyuge?*
What are the names and ages of your children?	*¿Cuáles son los nombres y edades de sus hijos?*
Who was George Washington?	*¿Quién era George Washington?*
Now, please repeat the three words I gave you earlier.	*Ahora, por favor, repita las tres palabras que le di antes.*

SEXUALLY TRANSMITTED DISEASES/HIV

This is not a lengthy section, but it is a very sensitive topic, and being able to explain what you are doing should help ease your patient's anxiety.

English Phrase	Spanish Phrase
PATIENT INFORMATION	
What brings you here today?	¿Por qué está usted aquí hoy?
What are your symptoms?	¿Qué son sus síntomas?
Is there discharge from you penis/vagina? Itching? An odor? Pain?	¿Hay un desecho de su pene/vagina? ¿Hay comazón? ¿Hay un olor? ¿Le duele?
Do you have a rash? Warts? Have you noticed a sore or sores?	¿Tiene usted una erupción? ¿Tiene usted verrugas? ¿Ha notada una llaga o llagas?
Does it hurt to urinate?	¿Le duele a orinar?
How long have you had those symptoms?	¿Cuánto tiempo ha tenido estos síntomas?
When was the last time you had sex?	¿Cuándo fue la última vez que tuvo relaciones sexuales?

English Phrase	Spanish Phrase
Did you have sex with a man or with a woman?	*¿Tuvo usted relaciones sexuales con un hombre o una mujer?*
Did you have anal sex, oral sex, or vaginal sex?	*¿Tuvo usted sexo anal, sexo oral, or sexo vaginal?*
Do you normally have sex with men, women, or both?	*¿Normalmente, tiene usted relaciones sexuales con los hombres, las mujeres, o los dos?*
How many sexual partners do you currently have?	*¿Cuántas parejas sexuales tiene usted actualmente?*
Do you use intravenous drugs?	*¿Usa usted drogas por vía intravenosa?*
Do you share needles?	*¿Comparte usted las agujas?*
Have you ever been tested for HIV?	*¿Alguna vez ha sido probado para la HIV?*

Note: HIV is translated la HIV. AIDS is translated la SIDA.

Have you ever been treated for a sexually transmitted disease?	*Alguna vez ha tenido tratamiento contra una infección sexual?*

PHYSICAL EXAM

I am going to draw some blood. We will check the specimen for syphilis and HIV.	*Voy a sacar sangre. Vamos a buscar la muestra por la sífilis y la HIV.*

SECTION 3

STDs/HIV

English Phrase	Spanish Phrase
I need to examine your genitals. Please take off your clothes, put on the hospital gown, and have a seat on the examining table.	Tengo que examinar sus genitales. Por favor, quítese la ropa, póngase la bata, y siéntese en la mesa.
I am going to touch your genitals.	Voy a tocar sus genitales.
I am going to take a sample from the tip of your penis. This will check for gonorrhea and chlamydia.	Voy a tomar una espécimen dentro de la punta del pene. Esta examen chequee para la gonorrea y la clamidia.
Please lie back and put your legs up here.	Por favor, acuéstese y ponga las piernas aquí.
I am going to put the speculum in the vagina so I can see the cervix.	Voy a poner el espéculo en la vagina para poder ver la boca de matrice.
I will do a pap smear and a test for gonorrhea and chlamydia.	Voy a hacer un examen pap y otro examen para la gonorrea y la clamidia.
I am going to touch inside the vagina with my fingers.	Voy a tocar al dentro de la vagina con mis dedos.
You have a yeast infection.	Tiene una infección de los hongos.
You have a urinary tract infection.	Tiene una infección orinaria.
You have a bacterial infection of the vagina.	Tiene una infección bacterial en la vagina.

English Phrase	Spanish Phrase
I am going to give you a prescription for some antibiotics to treat the infection.	Voy a darle una receta para antibióticos para el tratamiento de infección.
It takes several days to get the results of the tests for gonorrhea and chlamydia.	Se necesitan varios días para obtener resultados para los exámenes por la gonorrea y la clamidia.
Because of your symptoms, I am going to give you some antibiotics for gonorrhea, even though we don't have the results yet.	Dado sus síntomas, voy a darle antibióticos por el tratamiento de la gonorrea, aunque no tenemos los resultados todavía.
It is important that your sexual partner(s) be treated, too. They will need to see their doctor right away.	Es importante que sus parejas sexuales se tratan, también. Ellos tienen que ver sus doctores en seguida.
Do not have sex until you both/all of you have completed the treatment.	No tenga relaciones sexuales hasta los dos de ustedes/todos de ustedes hayan completado el tratamiento.
Your blood test is positive for syphilis.	Su prueba de sangre es positivo para la sífilis.
This is a preliminary test, and we will need to do a more definitive one, but we are going to begin treatment for syphilis now.	Esto es una prueba preliminaria, y es necesario hacer una prueba más definitiva, pero vamos a empezar el tratamiento para sífilis ahora.

English Phrase	Spanish Phrase
It is very important that we contact all of your sexual partners so that they can be treated too.	Es muy importante que nos comuniquemos con todos sus parejas sexuales para que ellos puedan recibir tratamiento también.
Syphilis is easily cured with penicillin.	La sífilis se puede curar fácilmente con penicilina.
Your blood test is positive for HIV.	Su prueba de sangre es positivo para la HIV.
There is no cure for HIV, but there are drugs that help to control the disease.	No existe una cura para la HIV, pero hay medicamentos que pueden controlar la enfermedad.
If you take the medications as directed, you can probably live a normal life for many years.	Si usted toma los medicamentos como se indica, probablemente puede tener una vida normal por muchos años.
Caring for yourself with HIV is a long-term commitment. You will need financial and emotional support.	El cuidado de si mismo con la HIV es un compromiso a largo plazo. Se necesita apoyo financiero y emocional.
I am going to refer you to a social worker, and to a special clinic for the treatment of HIV.	Voy a referirle a una trabajadora social, y a una clínica especial por el tratamiento de la HIV.
You have symptoms of herpes.	Tiene síntomas de herpes.

English Phrase	Spanish Phrase
There is no cure for herpes, but we can give you medications to control the symptoms.	*No existe una cura para herpes, pero podemos darle medicamentos para controlar los síntomas.*
It is very important for you to use condoms if your partner has not already been infected.	*Es muy importante que usted use los condones si su pareja no ha estado infectado ya.*

ABUSE

Although abuse can take many forms, we're covering the two largest topics, domestic abuse and sexual abuse.

English Phrase	Spanish Phrase
DOMESTIC VIOLENCE	
Do you think you might be in an abusive relationship?	*¿Cree usted que podría estar en una relación abusiva?*
Does your partner hurt or threaten to hurt you or your children?	*¿Su pareja la hace daño o amenaza a hacerle daño a usted o sus hijos?*
Does your partner hit, kick, slap, push, or choke you?	*¿Su pareja golpea, patea, bofeta, empuja, o ahoga a usted?*
Does your partner try to control whom you see or what you do?	*¿Su pareja trata de controlar quién puede ver o lo que hace?*
Is your partner very jealous?	*¿Es su pareja muy celoso?*
Does he force you to have sexual relations, or to do things in bed that make you uncomfortable?	*¿La obliga a tener relaciones sexuales, o hacer cosas in la cama que la incomoda?*

English Phrase	Spanish Phrase
Does your partner prevent you from talking with your family and friends?	¿La previene su pareja de hablar con su familia y sus amigos?
Are you afraid of your partner?	¿Tiene miedo de su pareja?
These are signs of an abusive relationship. I am concerned about your safety.	Estos son señales de una relación abusiva. Me preocupa por su seguridad.
Here is the number of the domestic violence hotline.	Aquí está el número de la línea directa de la violencia doméstica.
Please memorize the number or keep it somewhere safe so that you can call it if you need it.	Por favor, memorice el número o manténgalo en un lugar seguro para que puede llamarlo si sea necesario.
Do you want to go to the local shelter for abused families?	¿Quiere ir al refugio local para familias maltratadas?
There are laws in this country to protect you and your children from abuse.	Hay leyes en este país para proteger a usted y sus niños de los mal tratos.
Would you like to speak with a social worker?	¿Quería hablar con la trabajadora social?
Would you like to speak with the police?	¿Quería hablar con la policía?

English Phrase	Spanish Phrase
Please don't be afraid to tell you doctor or nurse about what is happening at home. Please let us know if you need help.	*Por favor, no tenga miedo a hablar con su doctor o su enfermera de lo que pasa en la casa. Por favor, díganos si necesita ayuda.*

SEXUAL ASSAULT

English Phrase	Spanish Phrase
Can you tell me what happened?	*¿Puede decirme lo que pasó?*
Are you injured?	*¿Está lesionada?*
Where on your body were you hurt?	*¿Donde en su cuerpo está lesionada?*
Are you bleeding?	*¿Está sangrando?*
Do you think you were raped?	*¿Cree que fue violada?*
When exactly did the attack happen?	*¿Cuándo ocurrió el ataque, exactamente?*
Where did the attack happen?	*¿Donde ocurrió el ataque?*
Was there penetration?	*¿Fue penetración?*
Were you penetrated in the vagina, the rectum, or the mouth?	*¿Fue penetrado usted en la vagina, en el recto, o en la boca?*
Were you penetrated by a hand, a penis, or an object?	*¿Fue penetrado por una mano, un pene, o un objeto?*

English Phrase	Spanish Phrase
Were there any witnesses?	¿Fueron algunos testigos?
Would you like to make a statement to the police?	¿Le gustaría hacer una declaración a la policía?
What did you do after the attack?	¿Que hizo después del ataque?
Have you changed clothes? Bathed? Eaten? Had anything to drink? Brushed your teeth?	¿Se ha cambiado su ropa? ¿Se ha bañado? ¿Ha comido? ¿Ha bebido? ¿Ha cepillado los dientes?
Did you take any medicines?	¿Tomó usted algunas medicamentos?
Have you had a tetanus shot in the last ten years?	¿Ha tenido una vacuna contra el tétano en los últimos diez años?
Have you had the vaccines for hepatitis?	¿Ha tenido las tres vacunas contra la hepatitis?
Have you been vaccinated against HPV?	¿Ha tenido la vacuna contra el HPV?
What do you use for birth control?	¿Qué usa usted para el control de natalidad?
I am going to give you some antibiotics to treat you for possible STDs.	Voy a darle algunos antibióticos para el tratamiento de infecciones sexuales.
Is important to see your doctor or visit your clinic in two to six weeks, to check for pregnancy and to make sure the antibiotics are effective.	Va a ser importante a ver su doctor, o a visitar su clínica dentro de dos a seis semanas, para chequiar para embarazo y que los antibióticos fueron efectivos.

CARDIOLOGY

English Phrase	Spanish Phrase
BASIC INFORMATION	
How old are you?	¿Cuántos años tiene?
Do you have any allergies to any medications? Food? Latex?	¿Tiene alguna alergia a algún medicamento? ¿Alimentos? ¿Látex?
What medications are you currently taking?	¿Qué medicamentos está usted tomando actualmente?
Has anyone in your family ever had a heart problem? What type?	¿Alguien en su familia ha tenido un problema del corazón? ¿Qué tipo?
Do you smoke cigarettes?	¿Fuma cigarrillos?
Do you exercise on a regular basis? How often?	¿Toma ejercicio de manera regular? ¿Con qué frecuencia?
Do you eat enough fruits and vegetables?	¿Come usted suficientes frutas y vegetales?
Do you eat a lot of high cholesterol foods, such as red meat or eggs?	¿Come muchos alimentos de alto colestero?

English Phrase	Spanish Phrase
Are you under any stress at home? At work?	¿Está usted bajo tensión en su hogar? ¿En el trabajo?
(If female) Do you still get your menstrual period?	¿Todavía tiene su período menstrual?
(If yes) Do you take any form of birth control?	¿Toma usted alguna forma de control de la natalidad?
(If no) At what age did you stop getting your menstrual period?	¿A qué edad dejó de tener su período menstrual?
Do you have diabetes?	¿Tiene diabetes?
(If yes) Is your blood sugar under control?	¿Está su azúcar de sangre bajo control?
Do you have a history of any other health problems?	¿Tiene usted historia de otros problemas de salud?

PAIN

Are you having chest pain or chest discomfort at this time?	¿Tiene dolor en el pecho o malestar del pecho en este momento?
(If no) Have you ever experienced chest pain or discomfort?	¿Alguna vez ha tenido dolor en el pecho o malestar del pecho?

English Phrase	Spanish Phrase
When you feel chest pain, do you also have other symptoms such as sweating, nausea, heart palpitations, or shortness of breath?	¿Cuando siente dolor en el pecho, usted también tiene otros síntomas como sudoración, náuseas, palpitaciones del corazón, o sensación de falta de aire?
Point to where you feel the pain.	Punte a donde siente el dolor.
Describe the pain. Is it dull? Sharp? Stabbing?	Describir el dolor. ¿Es sordo? ¿Fuerte? ¿Puñaladas?
Is the pain constant, or does it come and go?	¿El dolor es constante, o se va y viene?
Does the pain spread to any other part of your body, like your jaw, neck, shoulder, arms, or back?	¿El dolor se extendió a cualquier otra parte de su cuerpo, al igual que la mandíbula, el cuello, los hombros, los brazos, o la espalda?
How bad is the pain, on a scale of one to ten, ten being the worst pain you have ever felt?	¿Tan malo es el dolor, en una escala de uno a diez, siendo diez el peor dolor que usted alguna vez sintió?
When did you first experience this pain?	¿Cuándo fue la primera vez que sintió este dolor?
Did the pain come on gradually? Or was it sudden?	¿El dolor vino gradualmente? ¿O fue de repente?
What makes the pain worse?	¿Que hace que el dolor empeore?
What makes the pain better?	¿Que hace que el dolor mejore?

English Phrase	Spanish Phrase
Are you feeling any numbness or tingling? Where?	*¿Siente cualquier entumecimiento u hormigueo? ¿Dónde?*
What do you take for the pain?	*¿Qué toma usted para el dolor?*
Does it help?	*¿Ayuda?*

BREATHING PROBLEMS

English Phrase	Spanish Phrase
Do you ever feel like your heart is racing? Skipping beats? Pounding?	*¿Alguna vez siente que su corazón esta de carreras? ¿Saltando latidos? ¿Golpeando?*
Are you ever short of breath?	*¿Alguna vez se siente corto de respiración?*
What makes you feel short of breath?	*¿Qué le hace sentir falta de aire?*
What makes the shortness of breath go away?	*¿Qué hace que la falta de aire desaparece?*
What makes the shortness of breath worse?	*¿Qué hace que la falta de aliento se empeore?*
Are there activities you can no longer do because of shortness of breath?	*¿Hay actividades que ya no pueden hacerlas debido a la falta de aire?*
Are you taking medication to help your breathing?	*¿Está tomando medicación para ayudar a su respiración?*
Does the medication help?	*¿El medicamento ayuda?*

English Phrase	Spanish Phrase
Do you have difficulty walking because of shortness of breath?	¿Tiene dificultad para caminar a causa de falta de aire?
Do you have difficulty climbing stairs because of shortness of breath?	¿Tiene usted dificultad para subir escaleras a causa de falta de aire?
Have you recently gained or lost any weight?	¿Recientemente ha ganado o perdido peso?
How much weight have you gained? Lost?	¿Cuánto peso ha ganado? ¿Perdido?
Do you have any swelling in your face, hands, feet, or legs?	¿Tiene alguna hinchazón en la cara, los manos, los pies, o las piernas?
Have you ever felt dizzy or lightheaded?	¿Alguna vez ha sentido mareado o aturdido?
What made you feel dizzy or lightheaded?	¿Qué le hizo sentir mareado o aturdido?
Do you ever feel dizzy or lightheaded when you rise from a lying down or sitting position?	¿Usted se siente mareado o aturdido a levantarse de una posición tumbada o sentada?
Have there been any recent changes in your energy level?	¿Se han producido cambios recientes en su nivel de energía?
Are you feeling more tired than usual?	¿Se siente más cansado que de costumbre?
Do you ever get headaches?	¿Alguna vez ha tenido dolores de cabeza?

English Phrase	Spanish Phrase
What causes your headaches?	¿Qué causa el dolor de cabeza?
Do your hands or feet feel unusually cold?	¿Sus manos o pies se sienten extraordinariamente fríos?
Have you noticed a difference in the amount of urine you are putting out?	¿Ha notado una diferencia en la cantidad de orina que está poniendo?
Is this a recent change?	¿Se trata de un cambio reciente?
Do you have to get up during the night to urinate?	¿Tiene que levantarse durante la noche para orinar?
How many times?	¿Cuántas veces?
Do you take water pills?	¿Está tomando píldoras de echar agua?
At what time do you take your water pills?	¿A qué hora toma sus píldoras de echar agua?
MENTAL EXAM (BRIEF)	
Do you have trouble thinking clearly?	¿Tiene dificultad en pensar con claridad?
Do you laugh or cry easier than before?	¿Hacer reír o llorar más fácil que antes?
When did you notice a change in your thinking?	¿Cuándo notó un cambio en su pensamiento?
Are you taking medication that may affect your thinking?	¿Está tomando medicamentos que puedan afectar su pensamiento?

English Phrase	Spanish Phrase
Can you tell me what the date is? Where we are? Why you came here today?	¿Me puede decir qué es la fecha? ¿Dónde estamos? ¿Por qué vino usted aquí hoy?

PHYSICAL EXAM

I am going to listen to your heart.	Voy a escuchar su corazón.
Please breathe normally.	Por favor, respirar normalmente.
I am going to listen to your lungs.	Voy a escuchar sus pulmones.
Take a deep breath, please.	Respire profundamente, por favor.
I am going to check your nailbeds.	Voy a comprobar sus uñas.
I am going to check the pulses on your wrists.	Voy a comprobar los pulsos en las muñecas.
I am going to check the pulses on your feet.	Voy a comprobar los pulsos en los pies.
I am going to check your feet and legs for swelling.	Voy a revisar los pies y las piernas para hinchazón.
I am going to check your blood pressure.	Voy a chequear su presión arterial.
I am going to check your oxygen saturation level.	Voy a comprobar su nivel de saturación de oxígeno.